WHAT STUDENTS ARE SAYING ABOUT
Major in Success

"This book is so incredible that it made me feel I had the power to reach the dream job I want. Don't change a single thing. This book is very insightful."

DENISE LORD
New York, NY

"One of the BEST I've read on the subject. (And I have read a lot!!!)"

CAROLINE FRANCIS
Lexington, KY

"Inspirational. I cannot put this book down. This is just what 'want-to-be-successful people' need for guidance and direction. I needed this book ten years ago as a struggling freshman. I graduated and thought the degree was all I needed. Now I am back in school pursuing my dream career. Thanks, Patrick, for sharing the tips most people don't or won't."

DEBRA RUGG
Norfolk, NE

"One of the coolest books I have ever read, it kicks butt. I don't know what to say, but WOW."

ANGELA TONG
New York, NY

"I consider (*Major in Success*) my bible to getting the job I want. The book is excellent. I would recommend it to anyone!"

JEANNIE GORECKI
Cleveland, OH

"I have never written to (an) author before, but I truly enjoyed reading your book. It taught me so much, and I wish that I had found it a long time ago. When I read all the success stories that you included in the book, I got really excited."

VORATHEE SCOTT
Arlington, VA

D0520879

WHAT STUDENTS ARE SAYING ABOUT *Major in Success*

"This book was very inspiring. For the first time I read a book from cover to cover with no breaks. I just couldn't put it down."

ERIC ZACH
Lincoln, NE

"This is the first book I can honestly say inspired me. After reading it, I was excited about my future. I can relate to you!!"

MICHELLE NAVA
Vallejo, CA

"I love your book! It inspired me to do things I thought I would never do. I admire you a great deal. I never knew what I wanted to do until I read *Major in Success*. Now there is not a doubt in my mind. I can't thank you enough. This book is awesome."

MEGAN BASHAM
Dallas, TX

"Your book is one of the best I've read on how to be successful not only in school but also later on in my chosen profession. Your book has given me a tremendous amount of motivation to go out and do the things that will make me a valuable asset to my university and my future employers. Keep up the great work!"

DONALD GASTER
College Station, TX

"This is one of the most helpful books I've ever read. Because of this book I now have my major. I also have a great idea of what I want to do for the next four years of college."

CORRY HYER
Kingston, RI

"This book is one of the most fascinating books . . . I own. It gave me so many tips that I would have never received in any of my classes. I've learned more from this book than I have from any of my classroom textbooks."

FALGUNI PATEL
Kenmore, NY

"I just finished this book of yours and I must commend you. The last few chapters blew me away. And the "Focus" chapter kicked my ass. I've been trying to verbalize this idea about talent—that it's not something . . . you're born with. And you totally summed it up—if you just focus on what you care about, you become talented. That's so true."

SCOTT LEBERECHT
Cincinnati, OH

MAJOR IN SUCCESS

Make College Easier, Fire Up Your Dreams, and Get a Great Job!

5th EDITION

PATRICK COMBS

TEN SPEED PRESS
Berkeley

Copyright © 1994, 1998, 2000, 2003, 2007 by Patrick Combs

Ten Speed Press and the Ten Speed Press colophon are registered trademarks of Random House, Inc.

Library of Congress Cataloging-in-Publication Data

Combs, Patrick.
  Major in success : make college easier, fire up your dreams, and get a great job! / Patrick Combs. — 5th ed.
      p.   cm.
  Summary: "Revised edition of the bestselling guide for college students looking to discover their passion and make the most of their college years; includes updated resources and websites, the latest job market research, and new student success stories" —Provided by publisher.
  Includes index.
  1. College student orientation—United States. 2. Career development—United States. 3. Study skills—United States. 4. Success—United States. I. Title.
  LB2343.32.C65 2007
  378.1'98—dc22   2007016243

ISBN 978-1-58008-865-7

Printed in the United States of America

Cover design by Chris Hall
Text design by Jeff Brandenburg
Photography © 2005 by iStockPhoto

12 11 10 9 8 7 6 5 4

Fifth Edition

DEDICATION

From Patrick Combs:

To my mother, Nancy "Mom" Combs, to whom I owe my most excellent upbringing. Mom, you taught me the most valuable lessons of all—"You can be anything you want"; "Don't worry about your mistakes"; "Be kind to others"; and "Look it up, that's what I bought the encyclopedias for."

To Deborah Lowe, the world's best professor. Deborah, the gifts you gave me keep on giving from the pages of this book. Thank you for so much.

From Anton Anderson:

To my mom, Lee Anderson, for showing me I had wings, and to my dad, Gary Anderson, for making sure I used them. To my sister, Chelsea Anderson, for always believing in me. To my mentor, Alan Newman, for showing me what is possible in life. And to my fiancé, Sophie Cheetham, for encouraging me to always follow my heart.

CONTENTS

Special Thanks vii

Foreword by Dr. Jack Canfield viii

Preface—Looking Back x

Introduction xi

PART 1: DREAM JOB 1

Chapter 1:   On the Road to Greatness 3

Chapter 2:   Truly Passionate 10

Chapter 3:   Major Excitement 16

Chapter 4:   No McJobs! 18

Chapter 5:   Money Matters 25

Chapter 6:   Your Ultimate Life 31

Chapter 7:   The Six Big Fears 38

PART 2: ACTION PLAN 47

Chapter 8:   Great Escapes 49

Chapter 9:   Work Hard, Play Hard 55

Chapter 10: Never Mind the Grades 61

Chapter 11: Classes Worth Their Weight in Gold 68

Chapter 12: Success on Your Time 74

Chapter 13: Excel-eration Training 79

Chapter 14: A Major Shortcut 86

Chapter 15: Life-Changing Reality Checks 90

Chapter 16: Really Get Into It 94

Chapter 17: Show-and-Tell 101

Chapter 18: Going Pro 106

Chapter 19: School Without an Internship Will Get You Nowhere 114

Chapter 20: The Surefire, Nine-Step, Ultra Interview Plan 121

Chapter 21: Choices That Pay Off. 128

Chapter 22: Future-Perfect Planning 137

Chapter 23: Now Get out There!. 140

PART 3: HIGH OCTANE 147

Chapter 24: Focus—and Focus on What You Care About 149

Chapter 25: Make Bold Decisions. 155

Chapter 26: Commit to the Long-Term 159

Chapter 27: Break Through Your Failures 162

Chapter 28: Pay Yourself 10 Percent First and Always. 166

Chapter 29: Be Good to Others. 169

Chapter 30: Bon Voyage! 173

Bonus Appendix: Tips for Teachers, Artists, Exchange Students,
                and Athletes 177

Websites for Success. 180

More Ways to Major in Success. 181

About the Author 182

About the VIP Contributor. 183

Index 184

SPECIAL THANKS

My thanks to the following people: Lisa Marlow for helping me the very most. Mike and Anne, for your rock-solid support. Lisa Ryers and Jo Ann Deck for the book deal, great ideas, and great energy. Alexis Brunner, who helped make this book happen in good speed with a minimum of fuss. Lenny Dave for the comics and enthusiasm. Scott Edelstein for the agenting. John Marlow for the constant supply of good articles and good advice. Christian Haren for teaching me the difference between admirable and enviable. Michael Combs for Total Recall. And the following people for their valuable encouragement and help: Marianne Marlow, Donald Asher, Donald Casella, Ellis Gold, Deborah Sorensen, Tamy Snyder, Christa Neilsen, Andrea Kasten, Christy Svalstad, Rita Keilholtz, Jennifer Monges, Carol Dawson, Jessica Snelling-Defilippo, Sonia Borg, Jack King, and Joe Bove.

Thanks to the following people for sharing with me and contributing their inspiring stories: Michael Bates, Wendy Kopp, Veronica Chambers, Karen Socher, David Eggers, Gilman Louie, Tabitha Soren, David Greene, Andrew Shue, Chris Lindquist, Jennifer Scully, Michael Elliot, Marcus Allen, Darron Trobetsky, Alexis Mansinne, Charnae Wright, Jessica McNamara, Oscar Foster, Julia Hughes, and Sophie Cheetham. Thanks to Scott Sevier for help with the photos.

Special thanks to the people who beta-tested this book: Steve Montano, Brian Fields, Nancy Fields, Stephanie Yee, Butch Lovelace, Nancy Meutz, Dwayne Lee, Andrea Cheung, and Amy Francetic. Thanks also to the following people who helped me in some essential way with revisions to the original edition: Angela M. Klueber, Christina L. Graham, Liz Kearney, Gilbert R. Gonzales, Kylae Jordan, Ireneo Ray C. Pinpin Jr., Annie Wallace, Vanessa Arteaga, Tiffany Christine Marshall, Amy Evans, Patti O'Healy, Tatiana Armstrong, Spencer Baum, Dean J. De Milio, Peter Jackson, Josh Popowski, Aaron Wehner, Aaron Sherer, Jack Canfield, Troy Stende, Michelle Watson, and Julie Bennett; and my wonderful wife, Deanna Latson. Very special thanks to Anton Anderson for his instrumental help on the fifth-edition revision; Melissa Moore, the excellent editor of this edition; and to Chris Hall for the great cover.

THIS BOOK CAN TRANSFORM YOUR FUTURE

Foreword by Jack Canfield, coauthor of the *Chicken Soup for the Soul* series

You're about to read a book about true success—success in college, in your career, and in life.

But it's not your usual book about getting good grades and landing a high-paying job. For Patrick Combs, that's not nearly enough. And he hopes that once you've read the first few pages of this book, it won't be enough for you, either.

Major in Success is about living a radically successful life. This means landing (or creating) your dream job right out of college, or soon thereafter. It means living a life that brings you real joy, meaning, and satisfaction—not just a good-paying job. And, most importantly, it means starting to fulfill your dreams *right now*—not months or years down the road.

I know Patrick's approach and principles work, for several reasons. First, because people who follow Patrick's guidance radically succeed— in some cases beyond their wildest dreams.

Second, because Patrick has walked his talk. By the age of twenty-eight, he was already working at his own dream job as a speaker on college campuses, writing books and columns on the side, and living the life he had envisioned for himself.

Third, because Patrick has a well-earned and well-deserved reputation as a speaker and writer. He has shared his wisdom, encouragement, and energy with tens of thousands of students at hundreds of colleges and universities around the country.

And fourth, I know from my own experience that what Patrick writes is true. Of course, *Major in Success* wasn't available back when I was in college (though I wish it had been). Nevertheless— through intuition, grace, or blind luck—I was fortunate enough to have followed many of Patrick's principles, and they have made an enormous difference in my life. One of the most important of these, for me, was focusing on what I loved to do; another was persisting in spite of my fears and failures.

I'm living proof of how important these principles can be. It may surprise you to know that the first volume of *Chicken Soup for the Soul* was rejected by quite a few New York presses before finding a home with a small publisher in Florida. If Mark Victor Hansen (my coauthor) and I had given in to our fears—or had agreed with the unenthusiastic publishers in New York—none of the *Chicken Soup* books would have been published.

Fortunately, with *Major in Success*, you have the chance to benefit from everything Patrick has to offer. So turn the page and let Patrick show you how you can live your dreams, become the person you most want to become, and get on the fast track to your own greatness.

Jack Canfield

PREFACE—LOOKING BACK

This is the fifth edition of the book, and it's been (egads!) fifteen years since I sat down and wrote the first edition. This little book, which I wrote when I was twenty-five, has succeeded in ways I never imagined. It won book awards, it's been translated into several languages (none of which I speak—note to self, must learn to speak several languages), it's being used as a course text in universities (and high schools) around the country, it's been read by the equivalent of a small city full of people, and it's prompted throngs of people to write me and say something to the effect of, "I read your book, it changed my life, I got my dream job." (Usually said in a much more eloquent way, of course.)

The advice in this little book has done wonders for me as well. As I sit here today, I have not one, not two, but THREE dream jobs that not only enable me to do what I love for a living but also set me financially free. My three dream jobs: (1) inspirational speaker, (2) success coach, and (3) solo theater performer. My speaking career has taken me to more than one thousand universities and earned me a place in the Motivational Speakers Hall of Fame (who knew there was such a thing?). My work as a success coach has given me an online business through which I serve thousands. And my theater work (I do a comedic one-man show) has taken me on a thrilling ride around the world, all the way to Off-Broadway and to some pretty cool heights in the comedy world.

Why am I telling you all this?

I'm telling you because the advice in this little book, *Major in Success*, works, and if you work it, it will transform your life to a degree that perhaps you cannot yet imagine.

Truly,
Patrick Combs

INTRODUCTION

The college system assumes that knowledge is power. But knowledge isn't power. The ability to put knowledge to use is power.

This book was written for all the students who feel like the sophomore who said:

> *I came to college and thought it was going to teach me everything I needed to know. And I'm the kind of student who reads all my assignments, goes to class, really listens, and works hard at my homework. But two years into it I'm beginning to realize that college isn't teaching me what I need to know—just like high school didn't. And I'm afraid that if I don't do something different, I'm going to graduate with very little helpful knowledge.*

You can be as successful as you want. You can get your dream job and you can establish your ideal lifestyle. Throughout the pages of this book, you'll find proof of this in the stories of ordinary students who have gone on to get their dream jobs because of a few good moves they made while they were still in school.

But you are at risk! Consider these research findings.

If thirty-eight students enter college, 39 percent will expect to be millionaires by age forty. However, only eighteen will graduate, and after graduation:

- Average credit card debt for each will be $2,169, with student loans of $19,000.

- Nine will move back home.

- Nine will be underemployed.

> ❝ Success is living up to your potential. That's all. Wake up with a smile and go after life. . . . Live it, enjoy it, taste it, smell it, feel it. ❞
> JOE KAPP, *former professional football player and coach*

> ❝ Most of us have lives too small for our spirits. ❞
> STUDS TERKEL, *author and broadcaster*

- Eight will still be living with their parents more than a year after graduating.

- Almost all will work for a company, instead of for themselves.

- Average lifetime salary of each will be $40,387.

- Upwards of 70 percent will not like their jobs.

These findings may come as a shock to you because most students are under the impression that picking a suitable major, getting good grades, and completing a degree will result in a good job and a good life. But that promise is simply not true. Even people who graduate with honors are finding themselves in lives that are burdened by not so great jobs.

Simply put: College won't teach you how to fire up your career. Because you are at risk, *Major in Success* is loaded with suggestions that virtually ensure your getting a great job at graduation. It does so by

> **It's not good grades we're looking for, it's more of a personality type. We're looking for people who can think, lead, make decisions, and sell themselves.**
> *Business recruiter*

> **Nothing great has ever been achieved except by those who dared believing something inside them was superior to circumstances.**
> BRUCE BARTON,
> *author and politician*

> **Ninety-eight out of every hundred people working for wages today are in the positions they hold because they lacked the definiteness of decision to plan a definite position. . . .**
> NAPOLEON HILL, *author of*
> Think and Grow Rich

Duel of the non-marketable.

At a Glance. Copyright by Michael Saporito. Used by permission.

providing you with a simple, powerful success plan that will move you out of the "risk" category and into a good life.

Here's another bonus: *Major in Success* is designed to alleviate one of the biggest problems you and a million other college students face—feeling uncertain about why you're attending college at all.

Why are *you* in college?

People end up in college for a lot of different reasons: because they want a good education, because they wanted to get away from their parents, because everyone else was going, because their parents insisted, because it's what their siblings did, because they didn't know what else to do, and so on. But shortly into the first semester, many students begin to ponder the questions: Why am I here? Am I here to get good grades? Am I here to build a career? Am I supposed to just learn all I can from my professors? Or to get a credential?

Why *IS college the place to be?*

Ultimately, college gives you the opportunity to increase the *quality of your life*, both now and in the future.

Warning!

Unfortunately, a lot of students do little, if anything, to actively increase the quality of their lives while they're in school. Many students seem to think college is some kind of rehearsal and that they won't start improving their lives until after graduation. They don't seem to realize that life isn't a rehearsal—and neither is college.

From day one in college, your future resume starts to take shape whether you want to put anything impressive on it or not. Your career path begins, whether you're directing it or not. Even your future lifestyle starts taking shape whether you're consciously trying to shape it or not.

This means it's dangerous to be in college, just to achieve in academics. You may get good grades but still not get a good job. On the other hand, it is also detrimental to focus only on getting a job while you're in school because you'll miss out on the richness of your studies.

The most dangerous way to approach college is with the idea that all you need to do is pay your dues and get your degree. If you approach college with this mindset, you shoot yourself in both feet. After graduating, you'll discover that you were paying dues to get into a club of people who missed the point. The point is that you're not in college to work for

You will have to learn seven to ten different jobs to remain employable throughout your lifetime

❝ Everybody needs some inspiration,
Everybody needs some motivation,
mix it up with some imagination,
and use your natural gifts,
You've got natural gifts. ❞
Lyrics from "Natural Gifts"
by THE KINKS

your professors, or your parents, or anyone else. You're there to work for *yourself* and your future.

Working for yourself and for your future is the central focus of *Major in Success*. The book isn't just geared toward getting you a job. Neither is it geared toward getting you good grades, nor to make college fun, nor to expand your horizons, nor to help you develop your talents. It's not even aimed at helping you get the most out of college. *Major in Success* is set up to help you increase the quality of your life, during college and after college. Better still, almost every tip in the book is good for your career and good for your academics.

I'll describe how to set yourself up for success in detail, complete with step-by-step instructions, later on in the book. But here's a quick preview of what the *Major in Success* plan looks like.

1. Go to college

The first step to *Major in Success* is to go college because college really is the best place you can go to learn, practice, and make something of yourself. College is rich in resources, people, advisors, and learning tools. And in our society, a diploma is the piece of paper that gives you access to better jobs. On top of all that, college is a blast! I've heard it described as a socially accepted four- to five-year holiday from the "real world."

But yeah, yeah, yeah, you already know college is a good thing to do. Heck, you're probably in college right now, trying to avoid some homework assignment by reading this book. And you probably also know that college doesn't result in a great job for everyone. You've seen loads of graduates struggling to find meaningful employment. That's why there are three more steps in the overarching plan.

2. Discover what to do with your life

The second step to *Major in Success* is to pinpoint your passion and find a job and career that matches. The first part of this book will reveal the secrets to doing this. When you accomplish this part of the plan, you'll be well on your way to *getting* your dream job. Skip this step and you're a candidate for a job that doesn't engage your interests, in a word: drudgery.

College. Copyright by Dan Killeen. Used by permission.

3. Do things that get the ball rolling

The third step to *Major in Success* is to acquire the knowledge and experience that will *qualify* you for your dream job. The middle third of this book is ALL about easy steps that ramp up your life fast. As you accomplish these things, your confidence increases, your success speeds up, and your value in the working world goes through the roof.

> **❝** If your goal is to have your own life, don't lean up against a wall waiting for someone to recognize you. **❞**
> ANDREW SHUE, *actor*

4. Master the habits that make you unstoppable

The last step in the *Major in Success* plan is where the rubber meets the road. The previous three steps are like training and preparing for a race. In the last step you start running and truly winning. When you're at this phase in the plan, things will look very different. You'll have different options to choose from and you'll see many possible routes to your dream job. You'll also have acquired many of the skills, traits, and abilities that will get you to the job of your dreams—and ultimately provide you with a meaningful life.

> **❝** If you are who you want to be you'll make it all right You won't find a way to be free if you never try **❞**
> *Lyrics from the song "Life's for Living" by* JERRY WAGERS

As you can see, it's not a complicated path to success, but it does focus on what's really important: motivation, skills, abilities, resources, credentials, relationships, and your dreams. It's the same path that got many former college students where they want to be, including David Letterman, Katie Couric, Tom Hanks, Oprah Winfrey, Robin Williams, and Bill Gates. In the next part of the book, for example, you'll learn:

- What finally convinced Tom Hanks to pursue acting

- How Katie Couric got to the *Today Show*

> **❝** It is the first of all problems for a man to find out what kind of work he is to do in this universe. **❞**
> THOMAS CARLYLE, *essayist and historian*

- What David Letterman did during college to get his start in television

- What enabled John Singleton to direct his own movie just out of college

- How Jay Leno got past a major setback and ended up hosting the *Tonight Show*

- How David Duchovny finally figured out he wanted to be an actor

- The step Conan O'Brien took during college that put him on track to his TV show

- How football legend Marcus Allen overcame his biggest fear

In addition, you'll find inspiring stories of lesser-known recent graduates who did well for themselves by making choices you might see as possibilities for yourself. You'll learn about:

- David Greene, who ended up being part owner of a company because of one informational interview

- Sophie Cheetham, who pursued a dream opportunity working with an HIV/AIDS organization in South Africa

- Jessica McNamara, who got an amazing job right after graduation as a result of her senior year internship

- Veronica Chambers, who got her own column in a nationally circulated magazine during college by cold-calling from the New York phone book

- Wendy Kopp, who established a major national nonprofit organization just after college by turning her senior paper into a business plan

- Michael Elliot, who got his dream job in Hollywood with a quick trip to his career center

- Oscar Foster, an English student who got to live his dream studying (and surfing) in California for a year

to be nobody but yourself—in a world which is doing its best, night and day, to make you like everybody else—means to fight the hardest battle which any human being can fight, and never stop fighting.
E.E. CUMMINGS, *poet*

You don't need to read this book as a list of tasks you should be doing while you're in college. Instead, look at it as possibilities to explore in your own life. It is a reality that all of us can be great at something. And although the entire book is about succeeding both professionally and academically, let me repeat the underlying philosophy of *Major in Success*: **Do the things that increase your enjoyment of life.**

So start the book and enjoy.

> *To improve the golden moment of opportunity and catch the good that is within our reach is the great art of life.*
> SAMUEL JOHNSON, *author*

PART 1

DREAM JOB

A musician must make music, an artist must paint, a poet must write, if he is to be ultimately at peace with himself.

ABRAHAM MASLOW

CHAPTER 1

ON THE ROAD TO GREATNESS

You've got to get a kick out of whatever you're doing. I'd rather see you as a happy UPS driver enjoying your customers than a miserable senior accountant at a Fortune 500 company making $70,000 a year. You only get one trip around so you've got to enjoy what you do and who you do it with.

TOM PETERS, management expert

Think of the students around you. What personal characteristic do you think will make the difference between those who become great at something and those who never rise above mediocrity? Intelligence? Family background? Confidence?

The answer is surprising. Benjamin Bloom, a professor at the University of Chicago, recently studied 120 outstanding athletes, artists, and scholars. He was looking for the common denominators of greatness and mastery. The study concluded that intelligence and family background were NOT important characteristics for achieving mastery of a desired skill. The only characteristic that the 120 outstanding people had in common was **extraordinary drive**.

Extraordinary drive is the primary characteristic that powered Jay Leno through twenty-two years of stand-up comedy before being chosen to succeed Johnny Carson. It's the quality that took Jon Stewart from blowing it in his first stand-up comedy routine to his own hit show on Comedy Central. It's the key behind Oprah's rise from a childhood of poverty to an empire of influence. It's the primary quality that enabled filmmaker John Singleton to write three full-length movie scripts during college.

Extraordinary drive is exactly what you need to succeed. . . . Extraordinary drive is the magic ingredient that will make your dreams come true. . . . All you need is a little superhuman ambition and the

> *"* I never worked at anything that wasn't fun. If I had my life to live over I don't think I'd change a thing, except maybe to take up mountain climbing. *"*
> A. C. GILBERT, *gold medal pole-vault champion, 1908, self-made millionaire, and creator of the Erector Set*

> *"* Anything you do, you better enjoy it for its true value. Because people are going to second-guess everything you do. *"*
> BILL GATES

> ❝ Nothing great was ever achieved without enthusiasm. ❞
> RALPH WALDO EMERSON

> ❝ All our dreams can come true—if we have the courage to pursue them. ❞
> WALT DISNEY

> ❝ The will to win, the desire to succeed, the urge to reach your full potential . . . these are the keys that will unlock the door to personal excellence. ❞
> EDDIE ROBINSON, *college football coach*

> ❝ Most successful people enjoy their work. The real issue is not what's "hot" but what you like to do. ❞
> JEFFREY ALLEN, *writer*

pot of gold at the end of the rainbow is yours! Well then, maybe you'd like to know where extraordinary drive comes from. EXTRAORDINARY DRIVE COMES FROM DOING WHAT YOU ENJOY. Doing what you love. Going with your strongest interests. Striving for your deepest aspirations.

Why doing what you enjoy is so powerful

Doing what you enjoy propels you to success. How it propels you to success is simple. Success in any endeavor takes a lot of effort, and the key to a lot of effort is loving what you're working on. In the words of author and Stanford University professor Michael Ray, "You know that you are practicing your true vocation when you love all the hard work, responsibility, and tedium that goes with it."

Working in a career you love is ESSENTIAL to success. Yet, a 2006 survey sponsored by twenty-four leading U.S. companies of 7,718 American workers found that only 45 percent of workers say they are satisfied (33 percent) or extremely satisfied (12 percent) with their jobs. At the same time, a much lower number actually feel very "engaged" by their jobs. Only 20 percent feel very passionate about their jobs; less than 15 percent feel strongly energized by their work.

You don't want to get caught in the dull job trap that most people find themselves in. Work that you are very passionate about turns obligations into opportunities. It transforms chores into chances. It changes an uphill push into a magnetic pull. Passion and joy do for you what gasoline does for a car. On the other hand, ill-chosen work (work you feel pressured to do, work you settled for, or work you chose merely for ease or money) is like trying to drive your car on gas mixed with sugar—you may go a little way, but you will soon break down.

In the medical field there is a phenomenon known as Black Monday. It refers to the fact that most heart attacks occur between the hours of 7 and 8 AM on Monday mornings. I don't know about you, but Black Monday reminds me that it's essential to choose work you love. Life's for living, not for working yourself to death!

Passion gives you the power to work hard. It accelerates the development of your talents. It puts aliveness and meaning into your life. So as the poet Rumi said, "Let yourself be silently drawn by the stronger pull of what you really love."

I have personally learned what a strong difference focusing on what you enjoy makes. My first year in college, I had no sense of which subjects really interested me—so I ended up in many classes that bored me to death, one of which was Elements of Nuclear Physics. (Hey, it sounded impressive.) I quickly learned the results of trying to focus on things that don't interest you—I didn't even turn in my final paper, which was worth 50 percent of my grade! I wanted to be a good student, but I found the subject so uninteresting that I couldn't get the final paper done.

Luckily, a few years into college I discovered that I had a strong interest in new technology and high-tech toys. I loved to read about them, know about them, and be around them. I was an intern at Levi Strauss & Co., when my boss was assigned to set up a videoconferencing system for the company. Videoconferencing! That was a job I could enjoy!

We were at lunch when I overheard that he was going to be in charge, and my heart started beating fast, and my mind started racing with the dream that I could help on the project. When I got back to campus that evening, I searched for articles about videoconferencing. I spent the next seven evenings gathering and printing more than fifty articles. I went to the library and photocopied pages from six books. Then I studied the articles, organized them into a three-ring binder, and took it into Levi Strauss & Co. I set the big black binder on my boss's desk and said, "Maybe this will be helpful in that new videoconferencing project you're going to be in charge of, and I'd love to help on it if you need any." His mouth dropped open in amazement as he flipped through the many articles, and when he finally looked up, he said, "Well, you obviously know more about videoconferencing than I do . . ." (long pause) ". . . and you obviously have a lot of enthusiasm for the subject. How would you like the job as Levi's videoconferencing manager?" My heart probably skipped five beats. When I recaptured my breath, I gladly accepted the

> **"** You really have to work hard to let what you are come through. **"**
> OPRAH WINFREY

> **"** You can be just like me. Don't just pussyfoot around and sit on your assets. Unleash your ferocity upon an unsuspecting world. **"**
> BETTE MIDLER

> **"** God gave me a special talent to play the game, . . . maybe he didn't give me a talent, he gave me a passion. **"**
> WAYNE GRETZKY

> **"** If we did all the things we were capable of doing, we would literally astound ourselves. **"**
> THOMAS EDISON

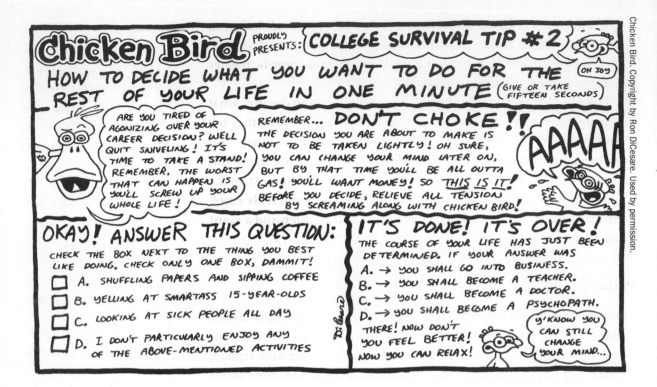

job, and he informed me that my salary would jump from $10 an hour to $25. I thought I'd retire in three months on that salary (at that time in my life my $10 an hour seemed high).

That is the power of doing what you enjoy! My love for new technology gave me the energy to do seven consecutive evenings of research. If it had been a subject I didn't care about, you couldn't have dragged me to the Internet or the library for unassigned research. In addition to giving me a tremendous amount of energy, my enthusiasm for the subject matter sent my boss the clear message that would have a lot of good energy for the position. Doing what you enjoy gives you energy and enthusiasm.

After college, it was my passion for speaking that powered me through the challenges of launching an independent career as an inspirational speaker, challenges that included being "too young," starting off as a bad speaker, lacking the right connections, and racking up $45,000 of debt. But passion powered me to true success in the speaking world. After speaking, it was my passion for performance that powered me through the challenges of making it in the world of theater and comedy. When I began, I once again lacked the right connections, was bad at

> ❝ Competitiveness is silly. There's enough to go around for everybody and fate is always, always working. ❞
> DREW BARRYMORE

what I dreamed of doing, and ran into roadblock after roadblock. But my passion was so great, it powered me through every obstacle and all the way to HBO, Off-Broadway, and a full-on career as comedic theater performer. Passion IS the key to success.

The problem is, most of us haven't been taught how to discover what we truly enjoy. As a man pointed out to me, "In other countries they tell you what to be when you grow up. In our country they only say, 'You can be anything you want.'" Well, how in the world do you figure out what you want to be? That subject is next. **But first and foremost, make a commitment to yourself to choose jobs and careers you truly enjoy and love. Your true commitment is the first essential step and a giant leap toward success.**

> ❝ We act as though comfort and luxury were the chief requirements of life, when all that we need to make us really happy is something to be enthusiastic about. ❞
> CHARLES KINGSLEY, *poet*

Discovering your best

I overheard a conversation between two students in a university library one afternoon. The young woman said to the young man, "We're out of here next semester—graduation came so fast." The young man replied, "Yeah, and I still don't know what I want to do for a job. How about you?" Her answer was, "I'm not sure either. I'd like to do something in communications, but I'm not sure what."

Wow, my friend, that is a bad place to be. Graduating without a clear picture of the kind of work you'd enjoy is like getting ready to skydive without a parachute—you're guaranteed a hard landing! You can't count on your college courses to reveal much about real-world jobs, so in the next chapter this book will walk you through the Quick-Fast, Usually Works, Four-Step Way to Figure Out Your Best Work:

> ❝ My advice is to live your life. Allow that wonderful inner intelligence to speak through you. ❞
> BERNIE SIEGEL,
> *psychologist and writer*

1. Admit what REALLY interests you.

2. Pinpoint your true aspirations.

3. Discover that there are many types of jobs that are related to your interest.

4. Feel your fears and do it anyway.

But first a cautionary story.

I delivered a speech about the importance of doing what you love at a conference in Chicago for students. Afterwards, a young woman came up to me and she was crying. She said, "Patrick, what if you don't know your passion? Or what if you're a person who doesn't have a passion?"

"I can show you how to discover your passion," I said. "And I assure you that you have one."

I grabbed a pen and paper and walked her quickly through the steps she needed to take to discover her passion. I thought she'd respond with something like, "Thanks, I'll try it." But she didn't. I was completely unprepared for her reply.

Looking down, she said, "Oh, maybe I don't want to know my passion."

I could barely believe my ears, but there it was. She didn't want to know her passion. I was so stunned and shocked by this that I began asking students at each college I visited if they could imagine why this gal didn't want to know her passion. The result was astonishing. College students everywhere named many reasons someone might not want to know their passion:

"If you know your passion, you might feel like you have to go for it."

"It might be something you're not good at."

"Your parents might be opposed to it."

"Your passion might be for something that doesn't make much money."

"You might need to move to another city or change schools for your passion."

"You might be majoring in the wrong thing for your passion."

"Your passion might take a lot of work."

"Your passion might take you way out of your comfort zone."

"You might not like your passion when you finally get it."

"You might fail at your passion."

"You might not feel you deserve to have your passion."

"It might be too late to go for your passion."

"Your passion might cost too much money to get into."

"Your passion might be too competitive."

ACHTUNG, BABY!

All of the above reasons are reasonable, common, and certainly choices many have made, but HEAR THIS: They are all, each and every one of them, the voices of fear. Therefore, they are poor reasons for turning your back on your passion. YOUR PASSIONS are the GREATEST TREASURES you'll ever find. They are a holy grail worth every step of the grand adventure they take you on. YOU WANT TO KNOW YOUR PASSIONS and you want to live them out fully, deeply, crazily, and completely. So, right now, take a deep breath and declare, **"I truly desire to discover my greatest passions and I am ready to have them revealed."** When you make this declaration with conviction, you enlist your higher mind as a powerful ally in your journey to discovering your greatest treasure.

Now, let's take the next step on that journey.

CHAPTER 2

TRULY PASSIONATE

Get excited and enthusiastic about your own dream. This excitement is like a forest fire—you can smell it, taste it, and see it from a mile away.

DENIS WAITLEY, motivational speaker

❝ I didn't become an actor to develop a personality cult or to get power over people. I went into this because it's fun, because it's a great way to make a living. **❞**
TOM HANKS, *actor*

❝ I really didn't know what I wanted or what moved me beyond basketball or sex. Those were two things that were very black and white to me, where I could feel in the moment. **❞**
DAVID DUCHOVNY, *actor*

In the awesome book *Before They Were Famous* by Karen Hardy Bystedt, actor David Duchovny, of *The X-Files*, talked about his college days. He was an A student and a good basketball player. "I was kind of drifting along, which might seem like a weird thing to say because I was seemingly doing so well. I was talented in a bleak way and I was just scared shitless that I wasn't going to be the best at what I was doing. But I didn't know what I wanted to do," he said. "From the ages of five to twenty, I'd always list that I wanted to be a lawyer or a doctor on all those tests they give you, but what I really wanted to be was a basketball player." But a basketball career didn't happen; his hands were too small, and after college he took a year off and bartended. "I applied for scholarships, thinking that if I continued to be a student I could somehow put off defining myself." Scholarships got him into Yale, but he went there still scared and undecided about what to do with his life. Then something happened. David made friends with Yale drama students and was soon inspired to write a play. "I started writing a play, and in order to learn more about writing I decided to take an acting class. In acting, I felt like I was playing ball again." His acting career started there, and within months he was in his first commercial.

Take note about a detail in Duchovny's story. He didn't figure out his passion for acting until he was in grad school. That brings up the most important point in this chapter about figuring out your passions:

MOST PEOPLE DON'T DISCOVER WHAT THEY'RE TRULY PAS-SIONATE ABOUT UNTIL AFTER COLLEGE, MUCH AFTER. THIS IS PERFECTLY FINE. BUT START SEEKING YOUR PASSION NOW.

I discovered my true passion for inspirational speaking at twenty-six years of age, four years after college. During college I was bouncing around like a pinball, interested in all kinds of jobs. If you figure out your dream job by twenty-six or even thirty you'll still be ahead of most. Don't worry if you haven't figured out your dream job. Instead, focus on taking the actions that will lead you to your discovery. Do this, and your dream job will find you.

The actions to take are quite straightforward and simple. But most of us have never learned them.

Do the passion pinpointer

First know that you're looking for your passion**S**, not your passion.

1. Know that a "passion" is something you enjoy. Yes, it's that simple.

2. Grab a piece of paper. Grab a pen. And list your top ten or twenty passions.

3. Recreational passions, academic passions, professional passions, personal passions—they all count.

4. Next, rate your passion for each on a scale of one to ten.

5. Then, choose your top three. (Don't sweat it. It's top three for today, not forever.)

6. Rest and have fun.

7. Repeat this exercise as often as needed. Each time you do it, you'll get clearer and clearer on your greatest passions.

8. Ultimately, you want to identify the things you could plug in to the sentence "I would love to _____!"

It is a very simple eight steps. The key is doing it and recognizing that some very obvious things about you are passions. The following can all be passions: music, fashion, sports, reading, writing, slam poetry, playing a musical instrument, performance, wine, conspiracy theory. Get it? Anything you really enjoy qualifies as a passion. ANYthing!

❝ More than anything else, people seek happiness. **❞**
MIHALY CSIKSZENTMIHALYI, *author of* Flow: The Psychology of Optimal Experience *(HarperCollins)*

❝ I was going to be a lawyer because that's what my brother was. But I worked in a law office and I hated it. **❞**
KAREN SOCHER, *president of Graphic Sound Records*

❝ I think it is possible to value yourself enough to say, my self is unique. There's never been anybody like me. Therefore, it is my duty on this earth to manifest that self in a unique way. **❞**
DAVID DUCHOVNY

❝ Life is short. Live it up! **❞**
NIKITA KHRUSHCHEV, *premier of former U.S.S.R.*

Another method for clarifying your passions is what I call the Magazine Test.

Take the magazine test

To get an immediate sense of something you're passionate about, look at the list of magazines in the margin (right) and pick the ONE you think would be the GREATEST to read for one year.

If there's some other magazine that you think of as the greatest, then so be it. In any case, when you've made your pick, you'll have a great indication of what you have passion for. The magazine you think is great might lead you to your dream job (more on that in a couple of chapters). The most successful people in the world choose a job based on how much they think they'll enjoy it. On the other hand, a lot of students will make the mistake of picking a job because it's practical—the equivalent of having to write research papers about a magazine you don't like forty hours a week.

One more thing on the magazines—it's what you would choose TODAY that matters. Don't worry about if it will be your next "passion of the month." Here and now are what matter when it comes to your passion.

A third way to find your passions is to . . .

Use your built-in compass

You have a built-in compass. It tells you with great accuracy when you're living your passions and when you're not. Your compass is easy to read and always with you. When you learn to use it, you will never be without a passion. You will walk confidently in the direction of a life you love.

So what's this built-in compass you have?

Your emotions are your compass. And they are wildly precise. Persistent negative emotions are good indicators of a lack of passion in your life. True South on this compass is perhaps boredom. On the other side, positive emotions signal that you are enjoying yourself and doing something you are passionate about. True North on this compass is definitely joy. You are constantly in a state somewhere between joy and boredom. Begin noticing your feelings.

Notice when you're really feeling good, enjoying yourself, excited, happy, engaged in what's going on, or deeply fascinated. When you are, you're passionate.

When it comes to living passionately, your own internal instincts are the best indicators you have. Trust your reactions—they are your best guides to enjoyment, fulfillment, satisfaction, and success. How did Tom Hanks know that acting was a passion? In his own words, "I signed up for a drama class and tried out for the plays, and got into them, and had more fun than I could possibly imagine."

When too many things inspire you

There is no such thing as too many passions or interests. The more the merrier, truly. Having a lot of passions can feel uncomfortable, but it's a good uneasiness. When Bill Gates, the president of Microsoft Corp., was in college, he had a very hard time deciding which subject was his favorite. In his own words: "When I was in college, it was really hard to pick a career, because everything seemed so attractive, and when you had to pick a specific one you had to say no to all the others."

The most successful people in the world have many passions, and often at the same time. The only difference between you and them is that they have learned to be okay with having so many passions, and they have learned how to prioritize their passions. So, if at times you feel overwhelmed by your passions, don't worry about it. You're walking in the same footsteps as most tremendously successful people. You don't have to throw out any of your passions, you just need to learn to slide some of them onto the back burner. Learn to go for your passions that have the most heat. Also keep in mind:

- College is a time for exploring as many passions as you can.

- Most of all, you want to graduate with an enthusiasm for learning. You increase your enthusiasm by exploring your passions. You decrease your spirit for learning by focusing on what other people say you should focus on. In other words, you'd be better off exploring your own passions in the library than sleeping through a class that bores you.

- Some of the most successful careers have been created by people who combined divergent passions in a new way.

Magazines:

Artist's Ways
Astronomy
Audio Video Interiors
Business Week
Cosmopolitan
Culinary Trends
Dance
Discover
Electronic Gaming
Farm and Ranch Living
Better Homes and Gardens
Martial Arts
Mother Jones
Money
Muscle and Fitness
National Geographic
Natural Health
New Music
Newsweek
Organic Gardening
Outside
Personal Transformation
Photography
Premiere
Road and Track
Sports Illustrated
This Old House
Traveler
Wired
Writers and Poets

- You will always be interested in many subjects simultaneously. Your job is to find ways to creatively combine your passions when possible, but also to work on them individually as time and focus permit.

- If you're overloaded with career ideas you'd love to do and cannot decide which one to pick, choose the bolder. Choose the path that takes more courage.

- Whenever you really don't know what to focus on, let a little time pass. Something will change or come up that makes your decision easier.

When your passions keep changing

In many respects, college is one big shopping center of passions. You may find yourself inspired by a new subject or activity every week. That's good! It's OK to have passions that constantly shift. Don't ever take your passions lightly. Become a master at knowing what your greatest passion currently is.

Still not sure what interests you

Some people struggle for a long time to come to a strong sense of what interests them. If it seems impossible to figure out what your interests are, go about your obligations, and your interests and talents will eventually reveal themselves. In the words of Goethe, "How can we learn to know ourselves? Never by reflection but by action. Try to do your duty and you will soon find out what you are. But what is your duty? The demands of the day."

Consider the story of Karen Socher, who graduated from UCLA. Karen remembers her confusion in college.

I spent a lot of time in the library looking for what I was supposed to be doing. I used to walk around the campus, reading all the flyers looking for something that would grab my interest. I saw so many things that were interesting, but because of my basic insecurity I'd think, "I can't do that—it's beyond my abilities." On top of that, I was lazy and wouldn't try things or give them a chance. I felt trapped in a rut where I wanted to do everything but I wasn't willing to do anything to get there.

There was no solution. I was miserable not knowing what I was going to do with my life. Everybody knew what they wanted to do, but I was just wandering around.

How, in light of her confusion, did she get involved in the music business and become president of the record label Graphic Sound Records, doing work she enjoys very much?

I was on the verge of just giving up. I was working as a legal secretary and getting really depressed. I'd think, "What am I doing with my life? Anything would be better than this!" I got so desperate that I took the first opportunity that came along—I volunteered to promote my boyfriend's band to talent agents at a three-day trade show. When the time came to actually go to the trade show, I was terrified. I'd never done anything like that before—put myself in a position where my performance could be judged. But I went through with it and I found that not only was I good at it, but people liked me. It was OK to be myself.

What was the single most important thing that she learned from all this?

You have to do footwork on everything. You have to take enough steps to get to a level where you can decide whether or not the activity is for you. Because otherwise you'll never know. If you're afraid and insecure at the get-go, you're going to assume that you don't like it without even trying it—without giving it a chance. And that's what I used to do. The trade show was a major breakthrough in my life. I was young, I was a woman, and I was enjoying some success at this big event. All of a sudden I felt like I became a special person. People gave me attention and I loved it! I walked away feeling like I could do anything.

Karen broke the cycle of indecision by grabbing an opportunity—in spite of the fact that she felt it was a risky one—and by doing the footwork necessary to experience a measure of personal fulfillment and success. Next, you're going to learn something super helpful for college: how to choose the perfect major.

HOT TIP: Check out *I Could Do Anything If I Only Knew What It Was,* by Barbara Sher with Barbara Smith (Doubleday)

❝ Don't feel guilty if you don't know what you want to do with your life. The most interesting people I know didn't know at twenty-two what they wanted to do with their lives. . . . Some of the most interesting forty-year-olds I know still don't. ❞
MARY SCHMICH,
columnist for the Chicago Tribune

❝ If everyone is thinking alike, then someone isn't thinking. ❞
DENIS WAITLEY,
motivational speaker

❝ I feel I'm successful mostly because I've become this person who wants to learn and grow—I think that's going to set me apart from the rest. I'm open-minded—totally looking at things around me to see how I can be better or how my business can be better—and I wasn't like that in school. ❞
KAREN SOCHER

CHAPTER 3

MAJOR EXCITEMENT

Everybody said, "Don't major in psychology; you won't be able to find a job where you can use it." Well, I did. I use it to get people to jump off a forty-foot crane.

RON SHERWOOD, employee of a bungee-jumping company

People can expect to change jobs 4.5 times during their twenties.
Bureau of Labor Statistics

HOT TIP: Sneak into upper division classes in a major you're considering to get a feel for what it is really like.

" It is possible to store the mind with a million facts and still be entirely uneducated. **"**
ALEC BOURNE, *author*

The ideal major is the one that you're the most passionate about. Colleges often overemphasize the importance of picking the "right" major, which makes choosing a major seem like a decision right up there with choosing whom you want to spend the rest of your life with. Although choosing your major can feel like a very big deal, it doesn't have as large an impact on your career as you may think.

For instance, Sue Coleman majored in behavioral pharmacology and now she manages mutual funds. Karen Socher majored in political science and now she works in the music industry. Richard Thau majored in history and now he works in politics. Margot Franssen was a philosophy major who went on to run the international business The Body Shop. Darren Star was an English major and he went on to create hit television shows. Let me spell it out: YOUR CHOICE OF MAJOR DOESN'T DICTATE WHAT CAREERS YOU'LL BE ABLE TO ENJOY.

First of all, choosing a major is not a major life choice. If statistical averages and present-day trends are any indication of how things will go for you, there's a 70 percent chance your first job will be related to your major. But after that, it's likely that your career will progress like a pinball. Many, if not most, people end up in all kinds of jobs that have nothing to do with their major. Let me put it this way—after your first job, your major becomes about as important as the classes you took in eighth grade, so you can knock "selecting a major" out of the Major Life Decisions category.

Second, selecting your major is not a rags or riches choice because employers aren't looking at your resume to see what you majored in. They're looking to see if you have the basic, practical skill to:

- meet deadlines

- work under pressure

- think critically

- work in teams

- write well

- use a computer

- manage your time effectively

- dress appropriately

If you don't have the skills listed above, you might as well have drawn yourself a Monopoly card that says, "Go directly to the underemployment line. Do not pass go. Do not collect $200." But if you do have these skills, you can major in whatever you want. Prove that you have these skills by taking the classes specifically recommended in Chapter 11, "Classes Worth Their Weight in Gold," and/or by getting work experience at a job or internship.

Seriously, if you want to design a special major all about European history, go for it. Employers will hire a European history major as long as she or he has also taken some classes and participated in extracurricular activities that demonstrate a competence in the tasks above (99 percent of employers are going to require that you've completed an internship, taken business-writing classes, computer classes, speech classes, etc.). Why would you major in something like European history? Because if European history is something you're passionate about, by focusing on it in college you'll enjoy your schooling more, and you'll increase your chances of ending up in a career that you absolutely love.

When someone says, "I don't know what really interests me," usually what they're really saying is, "My favorite things don't make for a good career." Wrong! There are many careers for every interest you have. So if that's what's holding you back from admitting what really interests you, do a clear and reset. Next, you're going to learn exactly how to link your passions and major to a real-world career that you can get excited about.

HOT TIP: Most graduates testify that if they had it to do over, they would major in whatever interested them the most.

75 percent of working America is in jobs completely unrelated to their major.

HOT TIP: You can choose a major that is "more likely" to get you a job at graduation, but often you won't like that job and you'll wish you'd just majored in what you thought was great.

Students ought to study anything that gets their creative juices flowing—definitely not something that only relates to getting a job. The most useful course I took was a humanitarian course on love.
MARGOT FRANSSEN, *former president, The Body Shop Canada*

CHAPTER 4

NO McJOBS!

Your profession is not what brings home your paycheck. Your profession is what you were put on earth to do with such passion and such intensity that it becomes spiritual in calling.

VINCENT VAN GOGH, artist

If you think that your interests just aren't practical enough, read the following stories about people whose true interests were considered as "impractical" as road-tripping, reading science fiction, exercising, playing video games, and beer.

Michael Lane loved most of all to go on road trips, so he and friend James Crotty launched a magazine called *Monk*, which they publish from their RV. The content of the magazine is basically their travelogue. Their circulation is national, and the magazine makes enough money to support their lifestyle.

- There are many job options for a person interested in traveling: travel writer, sales representative, landscape photographer, pilot, etc.

Rick Sternbach loved model rockets and science fiction when he was young and got a job designing the ships and gadgets you see on *Star Trek: The Next Generation*. He was also able to apply his interests to a previous job as a science fiction illustrator for magazines and books.

- There are many job options for a person with an interest in science fiction and rockets: science fiction writer, computer graphics designer, rocket scientist, etc.

66 Follow your bliss and be what you want to be. Don't climb the ladder of success only to find it's leaning against the wrong wall. 99
BERNIE SIEGEL, *psychologist and writer*

66 I learned never to give up from my dad. He taught me it's better to go after something special and risk starving to death than to surrender. If you give up your dream, what's left? 99
JIM CARREY, *actor*

Lisa Miller played volleyball for four years during college. She loved to exercise and stay healthy, so she took that interest and established herself as fitness director of a large fitness center.

- There are many job options for people interested in fitness: nutritionist, wellness teacher, professional bodybuilder, experiential education trainer, personal trainer, etc.

James Robertson has probably tasted more beers from more breweries than anyone. It's "his hobby." In every book he's written, six at last count, he's taken you on a tasting tour describing every beer he's ever tasted. By now he's tasted more than ten thousand beers. One of his books, *The Beer Log*, is more than six hundred pages, organized by continent and country. Robertson turned his interest in beer into a career as an author.

- There are many job options for a person interested in beer: author, magazine editor, brewmaster, distributor, marketer, even the entrepreneurial owner of a brew-your-own beer bar.

Chris Lindquist loved to play video games and after college he got a job as a game reviewer for *Electronic Entertainment* magazine.

- There are many job options for a person interested in video games: game tester, game designer, game programmer, arcade owner, virtual reality ride designer, etc.

Any and every interest can be turned into a successful career. If you can't think of jobs that would suit your interests or major, it's probably because of one of the following reasons:

1. You haven't consulted the ULTRA-INCREDIBLE series of career books put out by VGM Publishing. Do this: Go to an online bookstore and search for "vgm career books." You'll get a list of over four hundred incredibly specific career books like:

   Careers for Night Owls & Other Insomniacs

   Sports Nuts & Other Athletic Types

   Music Lovers & Other Tuneful Types

" Choose a job you love, and you will never have to work a day in your life. "
CONFUCIUS

HOT TIP: Great Websites to Research Potential Jobs:

- www.bls.gov/oco The Occupational Outlook Handbook

- www.jobstar.org JobStar Career information as well as current salaries

- www.asaenet.org Association Job Source Index of professional associations with excellent career info. Click "People & Groups," click "Directories," click "Gateway to Associations."

HOT TIP: Check out the book *Nice Job: The Guide to Cool, Odd, Risky, and Gruesome Ways to Make a Living* (Ten Speed Press). It has eighty-four job listings that tell you everything you need to know.

Mystery Buffs & Other Snoops and Sleuths

Travel Buffs & Other Restless Types

Born Leaders & Other Decisive Types

Cybersurfers & Other Online Types

Good Samaritans and Other Humanitarian Types

Opportunities in Animal & Pet Care Careers

Overseas Careers

Commercial Art and Graphic Design Careers

Cable Television Careers

Nonprofit Organization Careers

Performing Arts Careers

Visual Arts Careers

Beauty Culture Careers

Find the VGM book of your dreams and get it! Maybe it's at your library or career center.

HOT TIP: Found a potential company to work for? Read about them on one of the following sites to see if they are a good match:

• The Riley Guide, www.rileyguide.com (see "Tell Me About This Employer")

• Company Info Guide, www.virtualchase. com/topics/company_ information_index.shtml

• Google them!

2. You need to ask more people about possible careers.

3. You need to know more about the millions of career possibilities there are.

4. You're onto a job that a select few people go into and you'll probably enjoy a unique and interesting career.

I suggest you start by going to your career center or library and looking for *Job Hunter's Sourcebook: Where to Find Employment Leads and Other Job Search Resources* by Kristy Swartout, editor. If you don't find this book, ask a staff person to help you find something similar.

Ask as many people as you can what careers are related to your interest. Ask enough people and someone's going to suggest a great job that you never knew existed! A word of caution: Many people you ask will discourage you with statements like, "No such job exists," "It's not possible," or "I wouldn't recommend it." Thank them for their input and move on to the next person. You're on a mission, and you're going to have to pass a lot of people with limited vision and personal fears.

Try the job idea generator . . .

You can also get a real-world idea of possible careers by running your idea through something I developed called the JOB IDEA GENERATOR. It gives you a picture of the jobs that are possible for you. It may not give you the job specifics, but once you know the kind of work that is possible, you can easily look up the job title and company address on your own.

You want to know how it works? Fine . . . then stop right now and get out a pen. In the space below (or even better, in your journal) take what really interests you and answer the following questions:

- How could I be paid to inform people about this interest? (Perhaps through writing, consulting, speaking, TV, newsletters, magazines, shows, lectures, books, or computer bulletin boards.)

- How could I be paid to provide other people with a service related to this interest?

- How could I be paid to perform this interest for other people?

- How could I be paid to create products related to this interest?

- How could I be paid to assist people who are focused on this interest?

- How could I be paid to learn more about this interest?

If you did the JOB IDEA GENERATOR, you might be ready to call the career center or other knowledgeable professionals and ask them to help you with the specific job title/job description/salary range or the kinds of work that you identified as attractive. Or you can go straight to an INCREDIBLE book: *Professional Careers Sourcebook*. This book has everything you need to discover and learn about 118 professions. For each profession, it lists multiple career guidebooks, professional associations, test guides, educational programs, handbooks, newsletters, professional meetings, and even annual conventions. This book makes figuring out where to get important how-to information about your

❝ To waste any time doing something you don't really love is, to me, the ultimate waste of time. ❞
PETER JENNINGS

HOT TIP: Talk to campus experts such as professors, career counselors, and career conference organizers and speakers.

HOT TIP: Check out your university's online job database and career center. Often local employers will contact these offices before posting jobs to the general public.

Shocking Job Statistics . . .

- The average work year is 239 days. That's 10,755 days over a 45-year work period.

- 25 percent of Americans say the only reason they are at their job is because they can't afford health care coverage on their own.

- Only 13 percent of students go into a job they enjoy after graduation.

❤❤ I had an uncle who used to constantly ask me, 'Why don't you get a real job?' People always thought I was jerking around, and quite frankly, I wasn't making any money at it, so I'd even think, 'What am I doing with my career?' ❛❛
HOWARD STERN

career so easy to find that you might as well be taking cuts to the front of the line. I love this book!

Need some more ideas? Try the SUPER-SIMPLE, UNIQUE, & WEIRD JOB IDEA JOGGER! It couldn't be simpler. Fill in the blanks of the following sentence:

A great job would be [verb] in the [your interest] field.

For example, if you're interested in astronomy and you like to read, you get the sentence:

A great job would be reading in the astronomy field.

Reading in the astronomy field? What jobs does that make you think of? Hmmmm . . . Editor of an astronomy magazine? Researcher for NASA? Author of books about the latest astronomy developments?

Now change the verb to drawing and see what happens:

A great job would be drawing in the astronomy field.

What ideas does that jog? Hmmmm . . . Illustrating astronomy books? Architecturally designing observatories? Mapping star systems? Science fiction paintings?

Try this technique with your own interests and choice of verbs. You might be surprised at the unique and weird job ideas it jogs in your mind.

Enjoy yourself as much as possible

A lot of people might suggest that you choose a career based on your strongest talents. I caution you about choosing a career by asking the question "What am I best at?" You may happen to be good at something you don't necessarily enjoy. I'm really good at running, parallel parking, and typing. But I wouldn't enjoy being a marathon runner, a valet parking attendant, or an administrative assistant. I have no dreams based on those careers. Start from the activities you'd enjoy doing regularly and go get the skills required.

People will also encourage you to choose a boring, ordinary, safe job because they don't want you to fail. But remember this: Failure is a lot more likely when you're pursuing a career that you don't enjoy. Picture this: Two people working side by side, one out of obligation and one out of enthusiasm. Which one do you think is most likely to succeed? And which one do you think is most likely to stagnate, get passed over for promotions, dislike the job, and feel like a failure?

Somehow college makes it seem as if you should only aim for a career that fits into the category of Very Serious & Practical Work. That's fine if at heart you are a serious and practical person. But if deep down inside, you are very serious about having fun, don't let college erase your memory of all the jobs that fall into the category of Very Seriously Fun Work. Just in case you can't think of many fun jobs, check out the list of over sixty-plus unusual jobs that I've included in Chapter 18, "Going Pro."

And also remember that college isn't necessarily for getting an intellectual career. It isn't necessarily for getting a high-paying career. College is for developing your talents so that you can learn and do anything you like. When you start to focus on what you like, life starts to get really great.

If you want a really rare, unusual job

A lot of students dream of a getting a really cool, unusual, quirky, or high-profile job, but are hesitant to pursue it because the career path is narrow and undefined. Remember: The narrow path is more fun, it is more adventurous, and it is more rewarding. You were not meant to settle for a normal and safe job. You were meant to express yourself in a unique, exciting, cool way. You were meant to make your mark. You have urges and dreams about unique, exciting, cool jobs. Your destiny is speaking to you through those urges.

You can be the next one who makes it big but you have to practice, read, study, and learn. You have to commit to developing your raw talent into mastery. You have to be the first to recognize your star potential, and then be the driving force behind the development of your mastery. Your raw talent will turn into mastery if you polish your skills with persistence and passion. It is the only way anyone has ever "made it." For instance, a professional comedy writer is an amateur who didn't give up.

You'll hear many myths about jobs on the less-traveled narrow path. For instance: There's no guidance. You're likely to starve. The coolest jobs are one in a million. They require great talent. Simply put, these are all myths, lies, and b.s. passed around by people who let their fears get the best of them. Jobs on the narrow and less traveled path are: exciting

The universe does not send us a telegram saying, 'Do this, take that job; that's your soul mate.' The universe is more subtle than that. Simply notice what comes your way. If something comes up and it strikes a chord, put it in your back pocket and just let it be. Should it come up a second time, take it out and examine it, then set the idea someplace within easy reach, but still don't do anything about it. When it comes up a third time, LISTEN. The universe is talking to you.
DEBORAH NUCKOLS, *student, quoted in* Thinking about Thinking *by Clark McKowen*

My mother always encouraged me to pursue my work, and I don't think she's ever said, 'Why aren't you married?' Or, 'Hurry up, you're past thirty.' She's always been far more interested in creative pursuits than maternal and marital ones. And by doing that she's cleared away a huge obstacle that I think a lot of other women face.
SUSAN FALUDI, *writer*

and cool, envy-inducing, big-time rewarding, and AVAILABLE for the brave of heart, so go for it.

Sean Combs (P-Diddy) worked at Uptown Records, where he did grunt work like washing cars and fetching coffee just to get his foot in the door.

- The first step is to just get your foot in the door. It's OK if it isn't your dream job for the first few months or even years. It takes time.

Before Sheryl Crow's career took off, she worked as a backup singer for Michael Jackson and a songwriter for Eric Clapton, Tina Turner, and Celine Dion.

- Do anything you can to surround yourself with the people who are at the top of their game in your dream industry. Once you network with the right people and prove your value to them, the doors will begin to open.

50 Cent's first opportunity in the music world was collaborating with Onyx on the song "React" from their 1998 album *Shut 'Em Down*. He got the gig because Jam Master Jay of Run-DMC was impressed by his hard work.

- If you get an opportunity to advance your chances in your future career—take it! Prepare now and be the best you can be so you know that when the opportunity arrives, you will be ready to take the chance.

Read on because your life gets even greater when you follow your heart and let money follow you. . . .

" People can call me [a] madman, but when you think about it, the rest of the world lives in a box, gets into another box, drives off to work, then spends the whole day looking into another box. To me, that's masochistic. "
MATT PARRY, *traveling across America on a push scooter to benefit the homeless*

" Regret for the things we did can be tempered by time; it is regret for the things we did not do that is inconsolable. "
SYDNEY J. HARRIS, *writer*

" Do not follow where the path may lead. Go instead where there is no path and leave a trail. "
RALPH WALDO EMERSON

CHAPTER 5

MONEY MATTERS

Being rich isn't about money. Being rich is a state of mind. Some of us, no matter how much money we have, will never be free enough to take time to stop and eat the heart of the watermelon. And some of us will be rich without ever being more than a paycheck ahead of the game.

HARVEY B. MACKAY, entrepreneur and author

A Letter Home from College

Dear Dad,

$chool i$ really great. I am making lot$ of friend$ and $tudying very hard. With all my $tuff, I $imply can't think of anything I nccd, $o if you would like, you can ju$t $end me a card, a$ I would love to hear from you.

Love,

Your $on

> Out of one hundred 65-year-olds, only one will be rich, four will be financially independent, five will still be working, and fifty-four will be broke—depending on others for life's necessities.

Dear Son,

I kNOw that astroNOmy, ecoNOmics, and oceaNOgraphy are eNOugh to keep even an hoNOr student busy. Do NOt forget that the pursuit of kNOwledge is a NOble task, and you can never study eNOugh.

Love,

Dad

> ❝ We make a living by what we get, but we make a life by what we give. ❞
> NORMAN MACEWAN,
> *senior commander in the*
> *Royal Air Force*

Be true to your heart

Do you identify with a job that doesn't seem to pay much? Remember the words of Joseph Campbell, "Follow your bliss. There's something inside of you that knows when you're on the beam or off the beam. And if you get off the beam to earn money, you've lost your life. And if you stay in the center and don't get money, you still have your bliss."

Many people, including myself, have found that the best way to pick a job is by the amount of ENJOYMENT, SATISFACTION, and LEARNING the job has to offer. Consider the true-life story of Joy Greenidge, a field director for PLAN, a nonprofit that helps destitute children. Joy took a low-paying job with the agency and has enjoyed her work so much that she's passed up opportunities to move up the ladder and get paid more. What is her reward since it's not monetary? "In this job, no day is the same as any other," she says. "What can I say? It's been a wonderful life."

Jimmy Buffett, who's a celebrity musician, a *New York Times* best-selling author, and the founder of a successful restaurant chain called Margaritaville, was asked how he made so many successful decisions. He replied, "I remove money from the consideration. I ask myself, 'If money wasn't part of the decision, would I do it?' If it sounds appealing without money, then I go for it." A lot of people turn their backs on the career of their dreams because they think a low salary will make them unhappy. But beyond not being able to make a living, money has very little to do with happiness. Consider Jim Carrey's story. He was making several hundred thousand dollars a year as an impressionist when he reached a point where he really wanted to be recognized for having unique comedic talents. So much so that he quit doing impressions and walked away from an extraordinary income. His friends said, "You're insane. Don't do this." Jim said, "If it doesn't make me happy, what the f—k good is it? I'll have a lot of money and feel like an idiot."

Artists often pursue careers that are out of the mainstream and require an uncommon amount of sacrifice and risk. If this is you, by all means continue reading this book because its recommendations were written with you in mind. But because the arts are primarily not given their deserved legitimacy and proper place in our society, the following excerpt is exclusively for you. It comes from the book *The Gift of Giving* by Michael Lynberg.

> Money is an article which may be used as a universal passport to everywhere except heaven, and as a universal provider for everything except happiness.
> Wall Street Journal

> You must get money to chase you, but never let it catch up.
> DENIS WAITLEY, *motivational speaker*

> Why is there so much month left at the end of the money?
> JOHN BARRYMORE

> Money, it turned out, was exactly like sex, you thought of nothing else if you didn't have it and thought of other things if you did.
> JAMES BALDWIN

In your heart you may wish to be a painter, an actor, a writer, or a musician. You may be willing to give your life for your art, to sacrifice everything for creative excellence, beauty, and truth. This sacrifice may be necessary, for the life of the artist, while full of adventure and the thrill of creativity and discovery, can also be lonely and without the rewards valued by much of society. "Perhaps it will turn out that you are called to be an artist," wrote Ranier Maria Rilke in his Letters to a Young Poet. *Then take that destiny upon yourself and bear it, its burden and its greatness, without asking what recompense might come from the outside. For the creator must be a world for himself.*

Finally, a word for that part in us that can be determined to make good money. The following chart is to give you some proof that just about any job you're passionate about, no matter how odd, cool, or quirky, has awesome earning potential. If money matters to you, never forget that doctors, lawyers, and engineers aren't the only ones raking in the cash. You can follow your passion and make bank. (P.S. The real average salary of a lawyer is around $75,000. Good money, but then again, some rodeo clowns are making $90,000.)

The Mind-Expanding, Options-Enhancing, Eye-Poppin' Chart of OTHER Jobs That Make Big Bank

Airport manager	$130,000
Animation and digital effects background layout	$91,000
Animation and digital effects staff writer	$175,500
Antiques dealer	$50,000
Art dealer	$175,000
Art museum curator	$65,000
Athletic footwear designer	$130,000
Book publishing professional	$44,000
Brewmaster	$80,000
Camera operator	$46,300
Canoe instructor and coach	$45,000
CEO of a nonprofit organization	$100,000
Character animator	$106,900
Clergy, priest, rabbi, or minister	$62,000
Clothing/jewelry/cosmetics generalist	$41,000
Comedy writer	$80,000

> **“** Our income is like our shoes; if too small, they gall and pinch us; but if too large, they cause us to stumble and trip. **”**
> CHARLES CALEB COLTON,
> *cleric and writer*

> **“** Money is better than poverty, if only for financial reasons. **”**
> WOODY ALLEN

> **“** You should be looking for the joy, the struggle, and the challenge of work. What you bring forth from your own guts and heart. The happiness of hard work. No amount of money can buy that. Those are the things of the spirit. **”**
> JACOB NEEDLEMAN,
> *philosopher and author*

> **“** Money is good, but money shouldn't buy us. **”**
> ADAMU LAMU

> **“** Money isn't everything, but it ranks right up there with oxygen. **”**
> RITA DAVENPORT,
> *speaker and author*

" When I chased after money, I never had enough. When I got my life on purpose and focused on giving of myself and everything that arrived into my life, then I was prosperous. **"**
WAYNE DYER, *author*

" I don't want to make money. I just want to be wonderful. **"**
MARILYN MONROE

" Money is like manure. If you spread it around it does a lot of good. But if you pile it up in one place it stinks like hell. **"**
CLINT MURCHISON, JR., *founder of the Dallas Cowboys*

Commercial airline pilot	$200,000
Computer game designer	$78,000
Demolition contractor	$100,000
Diamond cutter	$150,000
Director of volunteers at a nonprofit organization	$84,000
Disc jockey	$40,000
Dog walker (in New York City)	$50,000
Environmentalist	$65,000
Executive chef	$75,000
Fashion designer	$50,000
FBI agent	$52,400
Film director	$160,200
Film editor	$70,000
Fire and crash rescue	$48,000
Firefighter	$50,000
Flight safety inspector	$85,000
Foreign diplomat	$54,500
Forest products technologist	$58,680
Forestry researcher	$70,000
Fundraiser	$46,500
Geologist	$50,000
Golf sales representative	$130,000
Graphic designer	$45,000*
Hazardous waste manager	$51,000
Helicopter pilot	$72,500
Hypnotherapist	$60,000
Interior designer	$60,000
Internet strategist	$115,000
Inventor	$90,000
Landscape architect	$53,900
Librarian	$54,600
Library director	$58,200
Lifeguard	$52,000
Lobbyist	$80,000
Magazine editor	$65,000
Magician (on a cruise ship)	$100,000
Massage therapist	$50,000
Midwife	$55,000
Motion picture art director	$115,000

Music talent scout	$80,000
Newspaper editor	$60,000
Organic farmer	$50,000
Philosopher	$60,000
Photo editor (at a magazine)	$60,000
Political campaign worker	$60,000
Politician	$90,000
Portrait photographer	$49,200
Private investigator	$60,000
Product name developer	$100,000
Radio news director	$102,676
Recreation specialist—aquatics	$40,000
Reptile keeper at a zoo (herpetologist)	$40,000
Restaurant critic	$75,000
Rock concert promoter	$48,000
Rodeo clown	$90,000
Senior high school principal	$66,600
Skydiving instructor	$42,000
Sports manager	$44,000
Stage technician	$45,000
Syndicated cartoonist	$100,000
Talent agent	$41,000
Toy designer	$58,000
Translator	$35,000
Travel writer	$72,000
TV news anchor	$200,000
TV news photographer	$120,000
TV reporter	$79,637
TV sportscaster	$128,877
TV weathercaster	$150,000
Wedding consultant	$75,000
Zoo director	$90,000

*Graphic designer is a prime example of the severe limits of this chart. I personally know designers who make six-figure incomes. Remember, your income can exceed what we've listed in this chart.

Sources: You name it, we pulled from it. We researched magazines, trade journals, institutes, surveys, and web pages. (We did, however, steer clear of using any writing on bathroom walls.)

" I know of nothing more despicable and pathetic than a man who devotes all the hours of the waking day to the making of money for money's sake. **"**
JOHN D. ROCKEFELLER

" It doesn't matter how rich or how poor you are, you can still afford to do the little, magical, ordinary things that make life great. **"**
R.C. DINI, *author of* How to Outlive and Out Do Every One

" Don't let your mind dwell on money at all, if you can help it. Throw yourself, body, soul, and spirit into whatever you are doing. **"**
HARRY B. THAYER, *former chairman of AT&T*

" Money doesn't worry me. All I care about is a good blue suit. . . . It doesn't even have to be good. **"**
WILL ROGERS

You may think to yourself, "Hey, these are much higher than the average starting salaries people have been showing me for my major. What's up with that?" Remember, it's not where you start—it's where you can end up! Starting salaries go up before long to numbers like those on the previous chart.

Money, money, money!

It's not a bad idea to look to those who've made a lot of money for advice and perspective. About money, Madonna said, "Money's not important. I never think, 'I want to make millions and millions of dollars,' but I don't want to have to worry about it. The more money you have, the more problems you have. I went from making no money to making comparatively a lot and all I've had is problems. Life was simpler when I had no money, when I just barely survived." Jerry Seinfeld said, "I don't really care about the money. In my business, the only way you get as much money as I have is if you don't care about money and you care about comedy; then you end up with money. I'm not the kind of person who could do a show and think, 'Well, we've kind of run out of gas here, but the money's great and the ratings are still good, so let's keep grinding them out.' That would break my heart."

A quick story to end the chapter. There once was a wise Zen monk who lived deep in the woods. People traveled from far and wide to see him. He refused no one. One day a young reporter decided to write the story of the wise man, so he paid the monk a visit. The reporter started with this question, "Of all the different people who come to see you, which do you prefer, rich people or poor people?" "Rich people," said the monk without hesitating. This surprised the reporter, who was expecting an evasive Zen answer about everyone being different yet equal. "Why rich people?" "Because," said the monk, "they already know that money won't make them happy."

OK, with a determination to follow your heart into a cool, unique, and rewarding job, you're ready for the best step yet. The exciting step. The step that makes it all worthwhile. The light at the end of the tunnel.

❝ If I ever get real rich, I hope I'm not real mean to poor people, like I am now. **❞**
JACK HANDEY, *humorist*

❝ Don't judge yourself by somebody else's standards. You will always lose. **❞**
BILLY CORGAN *of the Smashing Pumpkins*

❝ Work like you don't need money, love like you've never been hurt, and dance like no one's watching. **❞**
Lyrics by U2

CHAPTER 6

YOUR ULTIMATE LIFE

Visionaries are not special people. The gift of true vision requires only a willingness to open your eyes to first find the horizon. Once fixated on the horizon comes the ability to see beyond, where the true magic of life exists.

RICK BENETEAU, personal coach

As a kid, Conan O'Brien sat around the dinner table entertaining his family with jokes. He grew up and created a life for himself entertaining a national audience every night. Jane Goodall dreamed of living in Africa and writing about animals ever since she saw *Dr. Doolittle* at age eight. Jay Leno's two loves during his teens were cars and comedy—not only does he now do comedy every evening but he also has a large collection of exotic automobiles. As a kid, John Singleton watched movies on a seventy-foot drive-in movie screen outside his window and dreamed of being a moviemaker—now he's an established A-list director in Hollywood.

The testimonials that support following your passion to lead you to your dream life go on and on. Modern dance legend Martha Graham said, "My fate was sealed," referring to the night when she was seventeen and saw an incredible dance performance. Robin Williams described the year in college that he flunked out of political science but discovered improvisational theater. "Everything opened up, the whole world just changed in that one year." Oprah Winfrey hosted a talk show and liked it so much she said, "This is what I should be doing. It's like breathing." When discussing his success, David Letterman said, "All I ever wanted was to have my own television show." Michael Stipe, lead singer of R.E.M., said, "I heard Patti Smith's album *Horses* and it gave me, you

> ❝ Keep away from people who try to belittle your ambitions. Small people always do that, but the really great make you feel that you, too, can become great. ❞
> MARK TWAIN

> ❝ Greatness is a measure in one's spirit, not a result of one's rank in human affairs. ❞
> SHERMAN FINESILVER, *judge*

“ If you got up and asked how you could use your life to help others, your life would truly change. **”**
OPRAH WINFREY

“ You gotta live life for yourself
You can't live life for anyone else
You gotta live life that's all you do
Nobody gonna live your life for you **”**
Lyrics from "Live Life" by THE KINKS

HOT TIP: Carry a small pocket notebook with you to capture the thoughts you'd like to write about.

know . . . it gave me strength, it gave me incredible strength, and I knew immediately that that's what I wanted to do."

What if these people had decided to pursue something more "practical" or more "realistic"? Life is very generous to those who follow their passions and pursue their dreams.

We all have a destiny and it speaks to us through our passions and dreams. When you are clear about what you want out of life, it's easier to choose jobs you'll excel at and love. You can bring your passions and dreams front and center with a tool that is 99 percent effective, totally valuable, and unimaginably powerful: power journaling. Stop right now and apply a pen to paper or keys to keyboard and answer these questions:

- What am I excited about in my life right now?

- What am I most grateful about in my life now?

- What is it I have not yet done that I truly desire to do before I die?

- What action could I take today that would lead me to my dream life?

- What would I want for myself if I knew I could have it any way I wanted?

Why journaling is so powerful

Power journaling gives you the opportunity to answer powerful questions. Answering powerful questions gives you powerful answers. For instance, most students go through college constantly asking themselves, "How can I get better grades?" At best, this question will encourage your mind to come up with more ways to get A's. A more powerful question is, "What would I do if I knew I couldn't fail?" This question will produce answers about your dreams, aspirations, passions, and goals.

I got an email from a recent graduate telling me she had done all the things this book suggests, yet still didn't know what to do with her life. She was desperate for help. I told her I could help if she would email me some entries from her journal. She emailed back, "I don't journal. That's one thing from your book I didn't do." I wasn't surprised by her answer.

I've journaled since I was nineteen and it's been an incredible help. Journaling gives you clarity. In the book *Think and Grow Rich* by Napoleon Hill, the author challenges you to ask the first hundred people you meet what they want most in life. Hill says, "Ninety-eight of them will not be able to tell you. If you press them for an answer, some will say *security*; many will say *money*; a few will say *happiness*; others will say *fame and power*; and still others will say *social recognition, ease in living, ability to sing, dance, or write*; but none of them will be able to define these terms or give the slightest indication of a plan by which they hope to attain these vaguely expressed wishes. Riches do not respond to wishes. They respond only to definite plans, backed by definite desires, through constant persistence."

When you journal, you quickly become a 2 percenter who can clearly define what you want, name your definite plan, and be certain about your definite desire.

More questions that can change your life!

- What are the most important things in your life?

- What are the activities that you love and enjoy most today?

- What would be your ideal work environment today?

- How would your ideal work day go today?

- How would you define success today?

- What might be your purpose or destiny?

- How do you want to be perceived by your friends? Coworkers? Parents? Significant other?

- What magazine would you most like to be featured in for your tremendous accomplishments in ten years?

- What would you like to be the best in the world at?

- Who are your heroes and what is it about them that you most want to be like?

- What do you really, really think should be changed in the world?

> ❝ Show me whom you envy and I'll show you whom you ache to become. In determining what job a person would kill for, for instance, envy is far more accurate than any survey, horoscope, or aptitude test. ❞
> M. G. LORD, *writer*

> ❝ I live a life of curiosity and I get paid for it. ❞
> LARRY KING, *talk show host*

> ❝ A person with big dreams is more powerful than a person with all the facts. ❞
> DAYLE MALONEY, *philanthropist and author*

> ❝ Here's to the future! The only limits are the limits of your imagination. Dream up the world you want to live in, dream out loud, in high volume. ❞
> *Lyrics by* U2

HOT TIP: When you're in a job interview and they ask you if you have any questions, question them to find out which of your top five values the job can satisfy.

- What do you most want to be remembered for at the end of your life?

- Whom do you envy and what is it about them that you envy?

Know thy values

Also write about your values. Look in the side margin (right) at the list of workplace values and choose the five that you want most from a job. Base your answer on past experiences or simply on the way you feel today. Then prioritize your five choices, one being the most important value to you, five being the fifth most important. It's been said that if you don't know what you value most, you'll fall for anything. Meaning, you'll fall for a crap job.

The great thing about knowing your top five values is that you'll be able to decide whether a job is for you or not. It goes like this: If a job is going to satisfy only one of your top five values, every day on that job you'd probably find yourself thinking, "This job sucks!" If you get a job that meets two out of five, then it would probably be, "My job's OK, but I'd like to find something better." Three out of five, and you'll be thinking, "I've got a pretty good job." Four out of five and it's, "My job is awesome!" And when you hone in on a job that satisfies all five of your top five values, you'll be one of the fortunate few who can say, "I've got my dream job! I can't believe they pay me to do it!"

Tips on journaling

For starters, in a diary you mostly reflect on how your day went. In journaling you mostly write about how you desire your ideal days to be. Not, "My day went like this . . ." Instead, "Ideally my days will be like this . . ."
Also,

- Continually revise.

- Write when you're inspired.

- Write when you're reflective.

- Write when you don't want to make the same mistake ever again.

- Think big.

- Write from the heart.

- Write more from the heart than from the head.

- Work it, work it, work it—turn a one-paragraph answer into a page.

- Spell out your dreams specifically, right down to the smallest details about what you want.

- Describe your dreams accomplished in the most successful manner possible.

- Don't use the phrases "I want" or "I desire" or "I wish" or "I hope." There is only "I am" and "I will be." No one will read this but you. Be honest with yourself and don't be scared to say what you REALLY WANT in life!

Ultimately there is no right or wrong way to journal. There is only the act of clarifying your ideal life, defining your unique self, and—very important—having faith that it will all come true.

When I first started journaling I was hard pressed to come up with answers longer than a few sentences. But once I started, there was no turning back. My mind was engaged, and I began getting floods of answers at the oddest times. (Apparently my subconscious mind and heart were anxious to finally be heard.) I'd wake up in the middle of the night remembering an ambition I had almost forgotten.

An incredible detail of my ideal workday would suddenly come to me while eating lunch. A phrase or quote a friend or professor said would send me running to my journal. It's a process like this that transforms you from a person with loosely based wishes and dreams into a person with high motivation, passion, and a plan. It is a process like this that enables you to define who you truly are.

The weird, unexplainable thing about journaling

There is an even more awesome benefit to journaling, but it is discussed less often because it comes across like an episode of the *X-Files*. Journaling creates your reality. What you write about comes true quicker and often in seemingly strange and coincidental ways. On many occasions I have journaled one day about something I desired to come true, only to "coincidentally" meet the right person, discover the perfect resource, or

Workplace Values:

Achievement
Advancement
Adventure
Authority
Big dollars
Challenge
Charity
Choices
Control of your schedule
Creativity
Entrepreneurial
Excitement
Fast pace
Freedom
Friendships
Helpful to others
Helpful to society
High-tech environment
Independence
Learning
Less stress
Opportunity
Prestige
Pressure to perform
Recognition
Routine
Safety and protection
Security
Status
Structure
Teamwork
Travel
Variety

❝ All of us have a special quality or talent, a special vision or ability, that must be discovered and developed, that must be explored and expressed, if we are to live our lives fully. ❞
MICHAEL LYNBERG, *author*

> **" And you can dream
> So dream out loud
> And don't let the bastards
> grind you down "**
>
> *Lyrics by* U2

> **" The answer will hit, like
> a big psychic orgasm, if you
> listen to your dreams. They
> never lie. "**
>
> E. JEAN CARROLL, *journalist and
> advice columnist*

> **" Without passion you don't
> have energy; without energy
> you have nothing. "**
>
> DONALD TRUMP

> **" Did you ever try to pick
> a cold medicine? You stand
> there going, 'Well, this one is
> quick fast-acting, but this one
> is long-lasting. . . .' Which is
> more important, the present
> or the future? "**
>
> JERRY SEINFELD

> **" If you want something
> bad enough, the whole
> earth conspires to help
> you get it. "**
>
> MADONNA

UNABLE TO ANSWER QUESTION 23, "WHAT PERSONAL GOALS DO YOU HAVE TO GIVE YOUR OWN LIFE MEANING," FENTON PEEKS AT HIS NEIGHBOR'S PAPER.

get the perfect lucky break the very next day. One explanation for this lies in the truth that you must know what you want. Your unconscious mind has genius power to filter for, direct you to, and even attract things and resources that will help you create what you have said you want. Journaling makes you very clear on what you want and allows your subconscious to go to work.

Harvard Business School did an interesting study. They found that 3 percent of the American population had specific goals written down. Ten percent had specific goals, but not written down. Sixty percent had vague goals. And sadly, a full 27 percent of the population did not know the difference between a goal and wish. (A wish is a statement like, "I'd love to get a great job." A goal is, "I'm going to get a great job." It's the difference between believing you have control over your destiny or not.) The surprise of the study was that of the 13 percent who had specific goals, the first 3 percent who had them written down were more than ten times more likely to have their dreams come true.

Jim Carrey's story is a classic example of this mysterious power of writing down your dreams. Carrey went to Los Angeles to pursue his dream of being in the movies. He came from Canada and his family was so poor they were actually homeless for a while, but he was determined to make something of himself. One night in 1990 he got in his car and drove to the top of the Hollywood Hills so that he could have a better view of the city. While overlooking the city, he took out his checkbook and wrote HIMSELF a check in the amount of TEN MILLION DOLLARS; he postdated the check for Thanksgiving 1995 (five years later); wrote the words "Acting Services Rendered" in the memo section, signed the check and placed it in his wallet to carry with him. In 1995 he received his first humongous paycheck, a check in the amount of $7 million for his role in the film *Dumb & Dumber*. Later that year he was paid in excess of $10 million for *Batman*. "It wasn't about money. I knew if I was making that much, I'd be working with the best people on the best material. That's always been my dream."

Carrey's story illustrates a very deep truth. Your thoughts are creative. Turning your thoughts into words is even more powerful. Thoughts, words, and actions together are magnificently effective in giving birth to your reality. From the book *Conversations with God*, according to God, "You create everything in your reality. Life will take off for you when you choose for it to. Do you want your life to 'take off'? Begin at once to imagine it the way you want it to be—and move into that."

Journaling is a very effective way to get your heart talking. When you were a kid you probably listened to your heart more. For instance, in second grade I voluntarily entered a talent show and gave a monologue. Then in high school I stood up in front of all the students and ran the assemblies. Yet in college I forgot how much I liked speaking. It wasn't until age twenty-six that all my journaling reminded me that I truly loved speaking.

Every dream is worthy

One person's dream is to save the world, another's is to make a million dollars, and another's is to have a television show. It doesn't matter that their focuses are different, because each person has a unique destiny. It's just important that you are tapped into the dream that keeps you energized on the highway of life. (One note of caution for those whose dreams might be all about making money: Studies have shown that the more money a person strives to make, the less likely she or he is to be happy. A healthier alternative might be to dream about achieving mastery of certain skills that happen to make you lots of money.)

When you know your dreams and you know the subjects and work that really interest you, you are in the same starting position as the vast majority of people who go on to greatness. Now you need to get past your FEARS. Fear of competition, failure, lack of money. . . .

> ❝ One man has enthusiasm for thirty minutes, another for thirty days, but it is the man who has it for thirty years who makes a success of his life. ❞
> EDWARD B. BUTLER, *businessman*

> ❝ Build a dream and the dream will build you. ❞
> ROBERT SCHULLER, *pastor and author*

> ❝ Everyone who has taken a shower has had ideas. It's the person who gets out of that shower and does something with that idea who makes the difference. ❞
> NOLAN BUSHWELL, *creator of the Atari system*

> ❝ The mind is the limit. As long as the mind can envision the fact that you can do something, you can do it as long as you really believe 100 percent. ❞
> ARNOLD SCHWARZENEGGER

CHAPTER 7

THE SIX BIG FEARS

Pick a time and a place to deal with your fears or your fears will pick the time and the place, and they will deal with you.

DUNCAN BRASSINGTON

> **" So many times people end up fixated on doing things right, that they end up doing nothing at all. "**
> WRIGHT BROTHERS,
> *aviation pioneers*

Michael Elliot was a student I met after my presentation at the University of Arkansas. He grew up in a small Oklahoma town called Dewey. After his sophomore year he was planning to go back to the same summer job he'd had the year before, at a restaurant. It paid decent money and it was very convenient.

Six months after we had met he contacted me again. He said he'd left my talk thinking a lot about what he really dreamed of doing in life. It dawned on him that he thought Matt Damon had the coolest job in the world and he wanted to work in Hollywood. However, Hollywood was three thousand miles away and in a state he'd never been to. As a matter of fact, he'd never been outside of Oklahoma or Arkansas. To make matters worse, Michael had never taken any classes in film, acting, theater, or even creative arts. But instead of assuming his dream was impossible, he decided to take a chance.

He went to his career center to see if they had any Hollywood internships. He met with the unfortunate news that they did not. Instead of giving up there, Michael took another chance. He went to the library to see if they had any books that might help him find Hollywood jobs. They did.

Two days later, Michael was reading about Hollywood jobs when he got a call from the career center. They had just received an announcement for a summer internship at Miramax Films in Los Angeles. The news sent chills down Michael's spine. His first thought was filled with fear, "They'd never pick me." But then he thought, "I've got a one in a million chance of being the one they pick, but if I don't try, that puts my chances at zero." So Michael sent Miramax his resume and a cover letter.

Let me insert a brief comment here. I've personally met hundreds of students who have extraordinary jobs, and one thing has become quite clear. The people who get the coolest jobs are almost always the people who tried for jobs they figured they couldn't get. *Chances aren't given. They're taken.*

Michael took his chance and it paid off. "Somehow, someway, Miramax Films picked me," he told me. "It was the greatest time of my entire life! For instance, I was required—required—to go to all the Miramax premier parties. At one party, for the movie *Friday the 13th*, I found myself taking pictures with the star Jamie Lee Curtis." He went on, "Plus, I met some students in LA who were interning at Disneyland and before you knew it, so was I! Two dream internships! And then, at the end of the summer, as part of my internship, I went on two free cruises on the new Disney ship!"

I asked Michael what the greatest thing about his summer in Hollywood was. I thought he might answer "meeting the stars," "living in a big city," or "going on the Bahamas cruise," but he surprised me by saying, "Now I understand *it's reachable.*"

Your wildest dreams are reachable, but you must take chances, and taking chances means beating your fear. Had Michael Elliot let his fears stop him from going for his Hollywood dream, he would have settled instead for a repeat performance at the restaurant in Dewey.

All humans are afraid of something. There are SIX Big Fears in particular that usually stop people from pursuing the job of their dreams:

- Fear of poverty

- Fear of what other people expect

- Fear of competition

- Fear of choosing the wrong thing

- Fear of not having the right experience

- Fear of failure

There are others, for certain, like fear of not having the right major, fear of moving to a new city, fear of not liking it if it does come

> 44 The antidote to worry is purposeful action. 77
> BRIAN TRACY, *author and businessman*

> 44 Love your parents and teachers, but love your truth the most. 77
> CONFUCIUS

> 44 The real troubles in your life are apt to be things that never crossed your worried mind, the kind that blindside you at 4 PM on some idle Tuesday. 77
> KURT VONNEGUT, *author*

true—but naming all the different fears doesn't matter. Stiff competition, parental expectations, the wrong credentials, lack of connections, lack of experience, lack of money, lack of talent, and so on never stop people from reaching their dreams. There is only one thing in the world that stops people from reaching their destiny: Fear. Fear can and will stop you, *if you let it.*

I interviewed the one and only Super Bowl champion, Heisman Trophy–winning, MVP legend, NFL running back Marcus Allen. One question I asked him was, "What does fear mean to a person as accomplished as you?" His eyes lit up and he delivered his words like a fire chief teaching emergency instructions. "You have to collide with fear. You have to attack fear," he said, without flinching. He continued:

> *What I'm about to tell you, I'm more proud of than ANY of my football accomplishments. I've always been afraid of the water. Growing up in San Diego, my buddies were always going to the beach to play in the ocean. I'd always make up an excuse to not go with them, and I never went in the water. When I was thirty-six years old, I decided it was time to attack that fear, so I signed up for scuba diving lessons. Talk about facing your fears—I was suddenly sixty feet underwater and being told to keep calm while I shared my respirator with a buddy. Everything on the football field is easy compared to keeping your cool while you're sharing your air sixty feet underwater. But I attacked my fear and it opened up a whole new world for me. I do everything now: water-ski, jet ski, surf, scuba dive. But I never knew all I was missing until I faced my fear. Fear causes you to miss fantastic opportunities.*

And then Marcus Allen sent chills down my spine by saying, "That's the thing about fear. Death will kill you once, but fear kills you over and over and over, if you let it."

Five prescriptions for fear:

1. Feel the fear and do it anyway.

2. Get support from friends who believe in you.

3. Remember, you are equipped to handle anything that comes your way.

4. Know that F.E.A.R. is a False Expectation About Risk.

5. Replace your fear with faith.

❝ You gotta go get it. It's your life go live it. Round the corner give it some gas. **❞**
PAUL WESTERBURG, *singer/songwriter*

❝ Fear of poverty is, without doubt, the most destructive of the six basic fears. **❞**
NAPOLEON HILL, *author of* Think and Grow Rich

1. Feel the fear and do it anyway

You could call this the Marcus Allen school of thought about fear management. Attack your fears. Push through your fears. Feel the fear and do it anyway. The alternative is to let fear stop you, but then you'll have to deal with the regret of not even trying. Jim Carrey has a good story about feeling the fear and doing it anyway. "I've always tried to be somebody special. I used to go up to the Comedy Store to find something new.

   I promised myself that I wouldn't repeat a word I said the night before. Two-thirds of the time, it was garbage, but sometimes things would come out that were really kinda beautiful, and nice. That's the abyss, you know. You have to go right to the edge."

> 66 The real dividing line is passion. As long as you believe that what you're doing is MEANINGFUL, you can cut through fear and exhaustion and take the next step. 99
> ARLENE BLUM, *mountaineer*

2. Get support from friends who believe in you

The Beatles said it well when they sang, "Help! I need somebody. Help! Not just anybody. Help, you know I need someone. Heeeeeellllllp!" The CEO of Coca-Cola was once asked what he thought separated the ones who do OK from the ones who make it to the very top. He answered, "The ones who make it to the top are excellent at asking for help." When you have fears and insecurities about doing something, ask someone who believes in you, "Do you think I've got a chance of pulling this off? Can you offer me any advice for increasing my chances?" This will work wonders for your courage.

> 66 Gonna stand my ground, won't be turned around and I'll keep this world from draggin' me down, gonna stand my ground and I won't back down. 99
> *Lyrics from "I Won't Back Down"*
> *by* TOM PETTY

3. Remember, you are equipped to handle anything that comes your way

A fourth grader once said, "You have nothing to fear but homework." Think about it—have you ever not been able to handle a situation? When you face scary challenges where you risk failure or humiliation, what you're likely to find is that it's not as tough as you thought it was going to be. You have what it takes to make it through.

> 66 Fear is the only thing that can stop a person from reaching their dreams. 99
> PAULO COEHLO, *author of*
> The Alchemist

4. Remember, F.E.A.R. is a False Expectation About Risk

What you fear rarely ever happens. In his first few seasons, when ratings were low, Conan O'Brien feared his show was going to be canceled. But it's still going strong more than a decade later. Remember that Dorothy was scared of the great Oz until she pulled back the green curtain and discovered that her fears were unfounded. The fears you imagine are almost always just that—imagined.

5. Replace your fear with faith

You have a choice between living in fear or living in faith, and that choice begins with an understanding that fear and faith are just one word apart:

*Fear is what you think might go **wrong** but you have no evidence for. Faith is wat you think might go **right**, but you have no evidence for.*

So you see, it is just a one word choice between whether you live in fear or faith.

The more you realize that your fears are mostly imaginary, the easier it gets to replace your fears with faith. "The whole secret of existence is to have no fear," Buddha said. Fear creates insecurity, lowers your confidence, and silences your heart. Worst of all, it puts off bad vibes. It's been said that you attract what you fear. The more you can replace your fears with faith that things will work out, the more happy and powerful you'll be.

Here are some scenarios that may help you decide whether you want to pursue the career that you really want.

A. Possible Failure—So What?

- David Letterman's first television show was canceled due to bad ratings.

- At twenty-two, Oprah Winfrey was fired from being an anchorwoman because of her inexperience.

- The first time Jay Leno performed his stand-up comedy routine for Johnny Carson, Johnny told him he wasn't good enough for a spot on the *Tonight Show*.

- Lucille Ball's first acting coach recommended that she find a different career, and she was fired from her first four chorus-line jobs.

- Christina Aguilera appeared on *Star Search* and lost.

> ❝ Life shrinks or expands in proportion to one's courage. ❞
> ANAÏS NIN, *diarist*

> ❝ It is one of the great jokes of existence. Courageously journey to the center of your fear and you'll find nothing—just fear being afraid of itself. ❞
> PETER MCWILLIAMS, *author and activist*

> ❝ The only thing we have to fear is fear itself—nameless, unreasoning, unjustified terror which paralyzes needed efforts to convert retreat into advance. ❞
> MARTIN LUTHER

> ❝ The irony is that the person NOT taking risks feels the same amount of fear. The non–risk taker simply feels the same fear over more trivial things. ❞
> PETER MCWILLIAMS

- Mariah Carey started beauty school but dropped out and was later fired from her job.

"A person's ability to grow and succeed is directly related to their ability to suffer embarrassment," said Doug C. Engelbart, the father of personal computers. What Engelbart's quote implies is that mistakes and failure are necessary parts of achieving greatness. For myself, over and over I've had the experience of losing first and winning later. I was a bad long-distance runner before I was a good one. I gave embarrassing speeches before I gave highly praised ones. I made bad marketing materials before I made good ones. I wrote terrible cover letters before I wrote ones that won jobs. The moral of these examples is this: Yes, you might have failures along the way. But those failures are precisely what give you the feedback you need to succeed.

Worst-case scenario: You don't achieve the level you wanted to attain. But even in this case you are guaranteed to grow more than others who didn't take risks, and you'll network with many people who can be helpful to your future. Not a bad return simply for trying.

B. It's Your Life—Go Live It

Before Benicio del Toro was in *Traffic* and *Sin City*, his father strongly encouraged him to study business and become a lawyer. Del Toro secretly changed his major to acting and later moved to New York City to study the craft. Matthew McConaughey considered joining his father's oil business but decided to attend the University of Texas in Austin to study law. He changed his major to acting after reading the book *The Greatest Salesman in the World* and hasn't looked back since.

So somebody important to you thinks that your dream job is a really bad idea. Maybe it's your parents or a good friend. Here's a new way to look at it: Take their reaction as a good sign! In the words of career consultant Howard Figler, "You want at least one person to disagree with your career choice so that you know you're doing your own thinking." People who care about you will often discourage you out of love, not logic. They want to protect you from fears that are real to them but not necessarily true threats to you. If you're in this situation, do this: research the ins and outs thoroughly so you know the pluses and minuses better than those around you. If you decide it's worth the risks, tell the ones you love that you chose the career because you have more motivation

Tips on How to Feel Less Embarrassed:

1. Assume the people laughing at you wouldn't even try what you're doing.
2. Know that most people admire you for trying.
3. Remember that learning requires mistakes.
4. Be glad you're not on national TV (unless you are).
5. Think that the whole idea of "embarrassing" is lame.
6. Believe that it's healthy to get a daily dose of embarrassment.

66 We can secure other people's approval, if we do it right and try hard; but our own is worth a hundred of it. 99
MARK TWAIN

66 Follow your own bent, no matter what people say. 99
KARL MARX, *philosopher*

for it than for any other choice. Tell them that you researched the choice thoroughly and feel that it is worth the risks involved, and assure them that you didn't make the choice to hurt their feelings. Then Go For It.

C. Never Mind Your Major

Jim Conlon went to Syracuse University and majored in history. Less than one year after graduating he had a job with an investment firm. Jennifer Scully was an English literature/European studies major at Vanderbilt University. Two years after graduating she became the deputy director of trustee programs for the Democratic National Committee.

Uh-oh. You majored in business but now you wish you could be a fitness coach. Well, good news: Your major has very little to do with what jobs you can get. In a survey by the College Review Board, knowledge of your major ranked eleventh on a list of what employers look for. In addition to that startling fact, consider the words of career expert Dave Swanson: "Seventy-five percent of jobs are filled by people without the proper degree or qualifications." My personal testimony to the truth of that statement is the fact that my first dream job was as a technology manager, despite the fact that I had majored in speech and communications. And I currently write and speak about professional development despite the fact that I had no college experience in the field of career development. Your major and your work experience don't have to limit you. People often pursue their dreams in spite of not having the proper experience.

D. A Shirt for Your Back

Robert Kiyosaki didn't buy into the myth that it's impossible to be a teacher and make lots of money. He was flat broke when he started teaching at age thirty-two, and by forty-five he was wealthy and financially independent. In his book *If You Want to Be Rich & Happy Don't Go to School* (Aslan, 1993), he says, "Even Peace Corps volunteers could be millionaires if they comprehended the principles [of money making]." College will not teach you the principles he's referencing, but you can learn them for yourself by reading the short book *The Wealthy Barber* by David Chilton (Stoddart, 2002).

Does your dream job pay poorly? Don't let a low salary hold you back because there are many other ways to accumulate wealth. In addition to applying the principles for generating wealth that will make anyone on any income wealthy, remember to shop around because often the same job will pay significantly more in a different part of the country or world, or in a different industry. Finally, remember that above the level of being able to afford food and shelter, happiness has very little to do with income.

E. You Can't Touch This

Finally, if you're being realistic, you have to acknowledge the factor of competition. At the same time you have to acknowledge some other factors. First of all, consider the fact that we don't live in a world where you have to be the best, or even in the top one hundred, to be able to make a living at any certain profession. You wanna be a movie critic? You don't have to beat Roger Ebert to make a living at it.

Consider the enthusiasm factor. Maybe your dream job is very competitive, but you have more enthusiasm for that job than 95 percent of the other people applying. Enthusiasm is the greatest competitive advantage of all. Those working out of obligation run out of gas, while those operating on enthusiasm gain momentum.

Alan Kulwicki went into the astronomically competitive sport of stock car racing without any connections or money, in a sport that requires millions. He went about his goal with the attitude, "Maybe we can't win, but surely we'll lose if we don't try." Seven years after beginning his career he won the 1992 Winston Cup racing championship.

So, with new insights into the fears we all face, you are in a better position to pursue your true passion. Before I move on to a discussion of how to pursue your passions, you'll benefit from knowing two simple things:

1. People who have reached great heights were not fearless. (In fact, it seems that the ones who make it are the ones who can move forward despite having fears.)

2. In the words of Theodore Roosevelt, "It's not the critic who counts or the person who pointed out how the strong person stumbled or where the doer of deeds could have done them better. The credit belongs to the person who is actually in the arena; whose face is marred by dust and sweat and blood; who strives valiantly; who errs and comes short again and again; who knows the great enthusiasms, the great devotions, and

---

When billionaire Henry Ford was asked what he would do if he lost all of his fortune, he replied, "I'd have it all back in five years."

" A 'NO' uttered from deepest conviction is better and greater than a 'YES' merely uttered to please, or what is worse, to avoid trouble. **"**
MAHATMA GANDHI

" You'll always have the edge if you think you're number one. **"**
HARVEY B. MACKAY, *entrepreneur and author*

" Shut up and jump! **"**
Bungee-jumping phrase

" The most difficult thing is to just start the ball rolling. Once it starts, it's actually more difficult to stop it. **"**
BUTCH LOVELACE

spends themself in a worthy cause; who at best knows the triumph of high achievement and who at the worst, if they fail, at least fails while daring greatly, so that their place will never be with those cold and timid souls who know neither victory nor defeat."

> ❝ Mother can't you see I've got to live my life the way I feel is right for me
> Might not be right for you but it's right for me. . . . ❞
> *Lyrics from "Elsewhere" by*
> SARAH MCLACHLAN

In the next section of the book you're going to formulate your Action Plans. This is where things pick up speed. If your dream is to paint a masterpiece, you're going to start doing things that make you a great artist. If you're interested in helping people, you'll start taking actions that enable you to become great at helping people. If you're really interested in history and you dream of being wealthy, you're going to start doing things that will make you a high-paid historian.

But remember, the self-discovery process that you initiated in the previous chapters is a lifelong process that, when done with consistency, provides focus, motivation, and joy. Stay in the habit of journaling. Reread the previous chapters occasionally. Keep gaining clarity on what you'd like out of life. You'll stay in touch with the number one success factor: extraordinary drive.

PART 2

ACTION PLAN

Whatever you do or dream, you can begin it. Boldness
has genius, power and magic in it. Begin it now.

GOETHE, POET AND DRAMATIST

A Quick Pat on the Back

- Research has found that 58 percent of high school graduates never read another book from cover to cover the rest of their adult life.

- Approximately 78 percent of the population has not been in a bookstore in the last five years.

- The average child spends less than 1 percent of his or her free time reading and about 54 percent of their free time in front of the television (either watching it or playing video games).

. . . You are already way ahead of the game—keep going!

Rollin', Rollin', Rollin'!

With a clearer view of your interests and dreams, you are out of the starting blocks and on the track. In the next section of this book, you're going to learn:

- how to go on great escapes and get academic credit for it

- the most enjoyable way to gain real skills during college

- how to put your grades in perspective

- the classes that will save your a-- later on in the working world

- how to do more—better, faster, and easier

- how to make college work for you

- where and how to get leadership training

- the fastest way to become good at anything

- how to do reality checks that could change your life

- how to strike information gold when it comes to being an expert

- how a childhood game can improve your success

- how you can go pro with one phone call

By the end of these chapters you'll know enough to get more out of college than 95 percent of the students around you. The next chapter starts with the story of a student who went to the other side of the world to study at his dream university.

CHAPTER 8

GREAT ESCAPES

The man who has no imagination has no wings.
MUHAMMAD ALI

Oscar Foster, an English geography student, was ready for a change. Although he had a lot going for him at his university in England, his dream was to study in California.

> I had the chance to apply to other universities that wouldn't have cost as much, but I didn't want to pass up the opportunity of going to California. I was searching for adventure and the study abroad program presented me with this perfect opportunity! The year abroad was without a doubt the best year of my life. I met friends that I will have for life, experienced a new culture and lifestyle, and was exposed to a new method of teaching.

Oscar admits that the decision to go abroad can be quite scary and that there are a lot of unknown factors you will have to face.

> To be honest, the decision-making process was daunting. It was the beginning of the semester and I was already being forced to commit to my plans for the entire following year. What made it worse was that everyone else was choosing houses for next year, so if I didn't get accepted into the study abroad program I wouldn't get to live with my friends. And what was I risking all this for? Well, I didn't really know. Sure, we are swamped with American media and shows like The OC, but looking back on it there was nothing that could have prepared me for what I experienced. I was worried about the unfriendliness of foreigners, nervous about being an outsider and, of course, getting homesick. I finally decided I would never really know unless I tried it. And looking back on

HOT TIP:
http://studyabroad
.com is a terrific source
for a vast amount of
information about
studying abroad. Maybe
all the info you'll need!

it, I was never once homesick and everyone I met was really welcoming (they also liked my accent, which made a great conversation starter). If someone asked me to come back, I would jump at the opportunity. It was simply amazing. It was a gamble, but it definitely paid off!

As amazing as studying abroad can be, it is important to realize that there are some cons to the experience.

The hard part for me was being away from my friends and family back home. I went through a few period of culture shock, which I think is pretty normal and anyone studying abroad should be prepared for. One thing I didn't plan for was the impact on my school back home. While I was away, I missed some key courses that would have helped my final year.

If you haven't noticed up to this point, Oscar's overall experience was pretty positive. During his year abroad, he was able to join a university soccer team, he learned how to surf, he went to barbecues on the beach, tried to skateboard to campus, performed in open mic nights, and played guitar in a small local band . . . he really got out and took advantage of every opportunity. Above all else, what do you think the best thing about his experience was?

The best thing about my whole trip was meeting a new best friend. I know this sounds sappy but meeting new friends in general was the greatest benefit. I also learned to be much more independent and how to cope with unpredictable difficulties. I learned how to manage money and balance the beach with the grades. Above all else, the greatest reward was the new outlook the experience allowed me to develop on life. A year abroad is a life-changing experience. It opens up your eyes to a new way of living. Looking back on the experience, I realize how extraordinarily lucky I was to be given that opportunity.

Are you thinking about going abroad but not sure if it is something you want to go through with? Or perhaps you are interested but feel that you can't afford it or can't fit it in your schedule? Here is what Oscar has to say about that.

I say if you are thinking about doing it, go for it! Find a way and make it happen. True, you may not enjoy it, but you should never be scared to try something new. Every study abroad student I met loved their time abroad and would do it again in a heartbeat. If you do go, embrace

❝ At times [going abroad] won't be easy but trust that everyone and everything will still be there when you get back. **❞**
JULIA HUGHES,
studied abroad

❝ How could I turn down an opportunity like this? I would always regret not going, and even if I did go and it didn't work out, at least I had given it a go. **❞**
JULIA HUGHES

it with all your energy because the possibilities are endless. Enjoy the freedom and make the most of your time. Beware that the learning experiences in the first few weeks are sharp, but once you get past that, your time abroad will be an enjoyable rollercoaster and when you come out at the end of it, the feeling of getting through a year in a different country, environment, and social scene is so rewarding, there is no question that it is worth it.

Every student I've ever met who did a semester abroad remembers it as the single best experience they had in college. They describe the exciting travels they did to amazing places like Camden Market in London or the Indian Beer House in Taiwan or the Hamburg Fish Market in Germany or the Bastille in Paris or the Harajuku in Tokyo. Then, in the next breath, they mention the friends they made and the interesting people they met.

After hearing them talk about their experience, you begin to wonder if they went to classes at all! But yes, they did, and then they always have stories to tell about studying and school. For those who might be intimidated by studying in a foreign country, take note of what student Julia Hughes said about her overseas experience.

To be honest, it didn't really hit me exactly what I had undertaken until my plane landed and I walked out of the airport into the middle of a huge sprawling city. Just me, one suitcase, and no ticket home. This was it: me on my own for a whole year at the grand old age of nineteen. What on earth had I let myself in for? I felt a little overwhelmed by the crowds and the busyness. At first it is very easy to feel like a drop in the ocean. To my surprise, I got an overwhelming welcome from locals as an international student. Everyone was incredibly interested in where I was from and what my life back home was like. I couldn't have asked for more helpful, friendly, and welcoming friends. Looking back on it, the main benefit (apart from the tremendous amount I learned academically) was the overriding feeling of achievement: The sense that I did it, I made it, I came through unscathed all by myself; the experience I gained from being able to just take off and settle somewhere completely unknown and find my own path; and the ability to adapt to a different world but still remain the same person inside has given me a huge amount of confidence and faith in my own abilities.

❝ It's not necessarily the obvious differences that threw me off, sometimes it was just the little things like the way they expect the work to be laid out and the way the exam questions are worded. **❞**
JULIA HUGHES

❝ You can't possibly imagine what it will or won't be like or what will happen to you. Take opportunities, make the most of your experiences, and very importantly— enjoy yourself! **❞**
JULIA HUGHES

HOT TIP: Council on International Educational Exchange (CIEE) FREE guide to educational programs in the Third World contains a listing of programs in Africa, Asia, and Latin America. And there are grants available for those thinking about studying in one of these countries.

Amazingly, student testimonials don't end with travels, friends, and studies. Many students rave about the work experience they got overseas; some do office work in a city's downtown, while others do environmental work in a field in the country. Take, for example, California State University–Chico graduate Tim De Voe, who helped restore a habitat for waterfowl in the hay fields of Holland.

Our work provided continual opportunities to get to know one another and to share our cultures. Much of this took place in the flat-bottomed, open-air boat that helped us navigate the canal networks. Weekends gave us a chance to leave rural Holland behind and experience other aspects of Dutch culture. Highlights included a visit to a beach near The Hague (where swimming and sunning attire is definitely different than it is in the U.S.!) and to the National Park De Hoge Veluwe near Apeldoorn, where we gaped at artwork by Picasso, Braque, Redon, and van Gogh. Reflecting back on it, my experience at the work camp was one of the best I have ever had.

Add it all up and in the end why do most of them feel it was the best experience they had in college? One student, Trevver Buss, who studied abroad in Australia, summed it up pretty well by saying, "You'll learn the usual classroom stuff, but the education you get from the people and culture of another country can't be taught by a $50, ten-pound textbook with shiny covers."

On the other hand, how do employers look at overseas experience? They love it! And here's why: First off, it tells them they've found a person with a broad perspective. Having a perspective that is larger than a college campus or even a city is important to employers because companies now do business in a global economy. Employees who have global experience are just what today's companies need. It says to an employer that you have had experience adapting to new and unfamiliar circumstances. The ability to adapt to new situations is very appealing to employers because it tells them that no matter what changes come up in your job—people changes or responsibility changes—you will be able to adapt without too much trouble. That's a big deal to employers because many employees are not open to change. Last but not least, overseas experience tells an employer that you can deal with problems. One thing is for sure, not everything goes smoothly when you're studying or traveling in a country that is foreign to you. When employers see that you've been overseas, they know that you've learned a lot about dealing with challenges.

Benefits of studying or working abroad

- most likely some of the most fun you will ever have in your life

- amazing experiences you will never forget

- meet new lifelong friends

- encounters with interesting people

- increased self-confidence

- strengthening of a foreign language (if English isn't the primary language)

- weekend travel to other interesting places

- problem-solving skills

- time away from where you are now

- a global perspective

- dramatic improvement of your mind, abilities, and life

- great experience to add to your resume

> 66 It isn't what you know that counts; it's what you think of in time. 99
> UNKNOWN

> 66 You'll have a new way of looking at the world—and yourself—once you've adapted to a new environment and culture. You will open up a whole new world for yourself. 99
> TREVVER BUSS

How to Study or Work Abroad

Start by finding out if your school has a foreign exchange program (look in your course catalog or call an academic advisor). For instance, Rockford College in Illinois makes it easy for students to study for a semester at Regent's College in London, for no additional tuition or fees. This is often called a sister school relationship. In most cases, you'll receive academic credit from a sponsoring college or university and you'll be assisted and supervised by a resident staff.

If your school doesn't have an exchange program, check out http://ciee.org (Council on International Educational Exchange) for all the information you need to make it possible. Also make sure to get the latest issue of CIEE's magazine, *Student Travels*, as well as their *Work Abroad* brochure and a catalog of their many books. CIEE administers forty-one study abroad programs in twenty-one countries that are sponsored cooperatively by colleges and universities.

Each year, more than five thousand students (and recent graduates) work overseas through CIEE's Work Abroad program. Application procedures are simple—just fill out a one-page form. No minimum G.P.A. is needed, and for most of the programs, there is no language requirement. Typical job positions American students find include secretaries, chambermaids, office workers, hotel clerks, and fruit pickers. The pay is usually enough to cover your living expenses and enable you to go on a fair number of weekend excursions.

How Much It Costs

Whether you're studying abroad or working abroad, it's easy to cover your living expenses. Remember, studying and working are different from traveling abroad. Traveling is much more expensive. That's why it's best to see different countries through work or study programs. Costs may vary depending on what school you're attending and what country you choose to study in, but for the most part it's inexpensive (it becomes more expensive after you graduate). If you're there on a work program you'll usually make the same amount of money you'd make working in the States. Would you rather work in the same joint you worked in last summer or get off work and walk home through the streets of London?

My Own Regrets

I didn't study abroad and I feel like I missed out. I can't believe I didn't go—especially considering my college's many different study abroad programs, which I could have taken advantage of at very little additional cost. Now that I've heard so many of my peers speak so highly about their experiences, I really regret not having gone to study in London or Mexico. My friend David Thompson studied for a semester in Germany, and from what I can deduct from his postcards and stories, he had a much better semester than all of us back home.

Next, you'll find out how a twenty-four-year-old college graduate had the know-how to launch a big-time national magazine.

CHAPTER 9

WORK HARD, PLAY HARD

Enthusiasm is the match that lights the candle of achievement.
WILLIAM ARTHUR WARD, author

If you already know who Dave Eggers is, it's likely because of his success as a writer. His first memoir, *A Heartbreaking Work of Staggering Genius*, was runner-up for the Pulitzer Prize. His publication, *McSweeney's*, is quite renowned. And his most recent novel, *What Is the What*, has received critical acclaim. His status in the literary world could easily be described as gigantic. Before he became famous, I interviewed Dave for this book. He was twenty-four and the editor of *Might*, a magazine he'd launched with two friends. The first issue began with:

Yeah, yea. Another twentysomething magazine—who needs it? What is Might *and what does it want? And who wants* Might? *Who would read a magazine with a streaker on the cover? And where are the celebrities? The bands? The sex?* Might *is for young people, but there's no beauty tips, no dating hints or articles about partying. What gives? Where's the fashion? Where's the consumer guide? The fads? The models? The hype? The unreadable type? Could there really be more to a generation than illiterate, uninspired, flannel-wearing "slackers"? Could a generation really consist of 47 million different people? Could a bunch of people under 25 put out a national magazine with no corporate backing and no clue about marketing? With a shoestring budget and an unpaid staff? With actual views and actual issues? With a sense of purpose and a sense of humor? With guts and goals and hope? Who would read a magazine like that? You might.*

> **"** Often the writing I do sucks and it gets rejected. Just last week I did two illustrations where someone important told me, 'These are bad. Really, really bad.' It did hurt. You need pretty thick skin. **"**
> DAVE EGGERS, *author*

> **"** Diversify—don't put all your eggs in one basket. *SF Weekly* could call and say 'We hate your cartoon' and it wouldn't kill me because I have ten other things going on. **"**
> DAVE EGGERS

Dave Eggers wrote that introduction. On the side, he had his own comic strip running in a San Francisco newspaper and he was working on his painting abilities.

I make lists of things I want to do. For instance, years ago I put on my list that it would be great to have a syndicated cartoon or a published magazine. I'm trying to live as rich and as varied a life as I can.

Dave went to the University of Illinois and majored in journalism.

The University of Illinois wasn't my first choice. I imagined myself at an Ivy League school, but after I got rejected by Brown University and wait-listed by Cornell, I found myself in the cornfields of Illinois. It took me a long time to get used to it.

Being involved in extracurricular activities helped Dave settle in. Over the course of his college career, he got involved in several things: working on the campus newspaper, running the campus art gallery, participating in the campus concert promotions, taking art and design classes at Chicago Art Institute, and completing a summer internship at *Chicago* magazine.

I wanted my extracurricular activities and my summer jobs to advance my career. I saw a lot of students pick interesting majors but not think at all about what they needed to do in order to make their major practical. I was inspired by a visiting professor who, in addition to being a teacher, had an exciting career as a journalist and an artist. A fax would come in for him from The New York Times *with a design job. He'd cancel class, do the design, fax it back, and the next day you'd see it in* The New York Times. *On top of this, his art was being shown in different galleries around the world! Watching him, I learned that you have to work your ass off. And most importantly, I saw how much you can do, how many people you can touch, and how fulfilling it can be.*

So how did Dave get *Might* magazine started?

After working at a few different jobs after college, a high school friend and I just decided to do it. It was an idea we'd had for a while, and we were prodded or inspired by every magazine we'd see.

What made him think he could pull it off?

66 I think TV is great. When I'm in a hotel room, I sit there and try all these new channels and see what's going on. I probably stay up too late watching stuff. TV is neat. I don't have a TV at home, because I prefer to spend that time thinking—or mostly reading. So I'm pretty conscious about not letting myself get used to certain things. **99**
BILL GATES

66 I try not to leave things to chance. For instance, I like writing articles but instead of hoping that a magazine will publish them, I started my own. **99**
DAVE EGGERS

I picked up a lot of skills through my extracurricular activities in college, like computers, production, photography, and journalism, so I had some basis for my confidence. Of course, there have been a lot of obstacles, like raising the $10,000 we needed to do the first issue, but in the end it's "How bad do you want it?"

Extracurricular clubs and volunteer work are where the action is. They can provide opportunities to:

- meet and make great friends

- meet other people your age with similar interests and future goals

- learn a lot more about your interests

- start accomplishing your dreams

- gain the experience that employers and graduate schools look for

- do cool things like see guest speakers, put on events, work with money

- make a difference

- network with accomplished professionals

- take all-expense-paid trips to interesting conferences

- network to jobs in the real world

❝ We work sixty to seventy hours a week but it's fine, because for us this is work, leisure, and fun all rolled into one. ❞
DAVE EGGERS

❝ Bite off more than you can chew, then chew like hell. ❞
PETER BROCK, *race car driver*

Many tremendously successful people leverage their campus club experience into success. As you read about the other notable people whose stories are in this book, you'll find that all of them except one participated in campus clubs. And the one exception was Michael Bates, a student who was in and out of college in a total of two and a half years. So it's safe to say that campus club experiences have helped a lot of very successful people get where they are today.

For instance, shortly after graduating college Simon Tonner became marketing director for the computer book publisher Ziff-Davis Press. During his college days at San Francisco State University, he was the president of the advertising club. As an officer of the club he did many things, from making flyers to organizing fundraising events. But best of all, he and five other students from the club entered a contest to create an ad campaign for a line of Chevrolet cars. Together they made up a possible campaign, from the slogans to the commercials, and pitched it to a group of advertising executives from San Francisco. It's no wonder Simon got a great job in marketing after college—by the time he graduated he'd already gotten some real experience.

If advertising doesn't turn your crank, imagine having this experience next semester: you attend a three-day conference in a different city where hundreds of other students are also in attendance. There you take skill-building workshops; watch comedians, musicians, jugglers, sword duelers, hypnotists, psychics, motivational speakers, and fire eaters perform; and then schedule your favorite performers for a show at your school. In many colleges, students who are involved in the student activities club do this—and more—every year.

Campus clubs give you more than just great experience—they give you *connections*. Michael Minjares, coordinator for student enrichment at San Diego State, sees this happen all the time. He told me about Stephanie, a student who worked in the summer as an orientation leader assisting new students and their parents. One day while working the parent program, Stephanie was talking about life as a business major and her future career plans. It just so happened that in the parent audience was a gentleman who was involved in the same organization Stephanie desired to join. Impressed with Stephanie's communication and leadership skills, the parent approached Stephanie immediately after the presentation to offer her a business card and a chance to interview with his company. Booya! Why didn't someone tell me how GREAT it is to get involved in campus clubs?!

Find out what clubs and volunteer programs your campus has. Ask at the counseling center or look in the course catalog. You're likely to find many organizations that match your interests. For instance:

Accounting	Community health
Advertising	Economics
Agriculture	Environmental clubs
AIDS programs	Homeless shelters
Alcohol awareness	Hospital care
Art	Journalism
Children's centers	Marketing
Clubs that serve a specific ethnicity	Nursing homes
Photography	Student government

HOT TIP: Don't subject yourself to anyone who doesn't believe in, or encourage you to go all the way with, your ambitions.

Planned Parenthood	Student orientation
Radio	Teaching
Red Cross	Theater
Social work	Women's issues
Student activities	Writing

This is just a sample list. In case your school doesn't have the club you'd like to be in, remember you can start your own. Schools always have procedures for helping students start up a new club.

Great lines for your resume!

Students consistently report that being involved in student organizations was one of the most enjoyable things they did in college. But enjoying college more isn't the only benefit; there are also benefits for your future employment. As you learned in the first section of this book, employers are looking for a lot more than good grades and a degree these days. Extracurricular involvement is one thing employers love to see, and your resume will shine with lines like these after you've been involved.

- "Managed revenues and funds. Developed and implemented programs to promote diversity education" (for those who were involved in a campus club that educated the student body).

- "Counseled, aided, and advised new students" (for those who got involved in freshman orientation).

- "Planned and coordinated weekly meetings involving up to forty students and a guest speaker from the business community" (for those who planned meetings that included guest speakers).

- "Coordinated annual banquet" (for those who planned the end-of-the-year party).

- "Created and developed organizational selection recruitment and publicity" (for those who made posters and flyers and placed ads in the campus newspaper to get students to join club/organization).

- "Developed and implemented organizational selection procedures" (for those who planned the selection of new members).

> **In today's economy there are no experts, no 'best and brightest' with all the answers. It's up to each one of us. The only way to screw up is to not try anything.**
> TOM PETERS, *management expert*

> **Opportunity is missed by most people because it is dressed in overalls and looks like work.**
> THOMAS EDISON

- "Coordinated major public events, including national acts such as comedian Rob Schneider and rock band the Kinks. Comanaged $50,000 budget" (for those who were involved in student activities).

In a nutshell, after you've joined a campus club, your experience will say to an employer:

- This person is well rounded.

- This person has some real experience that will help him or her on the job.

- This person is self-motivated.

- This person can work in teams.

- This person may or may not have a pet. (Just checking your reflexes.)

- This person is an action taker and goes above mediocrity.

Make it work for your dreams

Use campus club involvement to accomplish your dreams. If your dream is to improve race relations in the world, then get involved in, or start, a campus club that focuses on improving race relations on your campus. This is how you'll find other people that share your dream. This is where you get resources like money, people, information, and connections. If what you think should be changed in the world is better treatment of the elderly, then volunteer at a nursing home. The day you start volunteering is the day the treatment of elderly people gets a little bit better. It's also the day you move one step closer to reaching your dream on a large scale.

In case you were wondering how it would be humanly possible to be active in campus clubs while also maintaining that dean's list G.P.A., next you'll read about a college student who didn't think getting straight A's was very important and who went on to be CEO of a $12 million company.

CHAPTER 10

NEVER MIND THE GRADES

Never let your schooling get in the way of your education.

MARK TWAIN

Michael Bates is rich at twenty-nine, but money isn't what motivates him.

I'll work around the clock on problems that are challenging, things that other people think can't be done, because for me, that's the ultimate fun. As for money, it comes when you're endeavoring to do your best at what you enjoy. And of course it's fun to make a lot of money, but it's not just money that makes me happy. The best part of my life is getting to work with a team of people that I admire and respect, who are focused on the same goals.

Michael went to college at Arizona State University and graduated with a mediocre grade point average of about 2.5.

I have a short attention span. I get bored very easily, and I can't spell worth a darn. But I'd find ways around my weaknesses to get papers done. I'd get a buddy of mine who was a good speller to type our papers while I'd dictate them.

Actually, Michael's G.P.A. wasn't an overriding concern because his focus was elsewhere: Starting up his own business of buying and selling used cars for a profit.

If I saw an opportunity, I took it. I was importing Mercedes and Porsches from Europe and buying and selling used cars. Used cars were 40 percent cheaper in Europe, and all I had to do was modify a few things and I could sell them for a profit.

> ❝ What you major in during college has no bearing on what careers you can do afterwards. ❞
> MICHAEL BATES, *entrepreneur*

> ❝ I've bombed in several businesses. The first software company I was in I made the mistake of signing personal guarantees for advertising and promotion. When the company went belly up they came after me for hundreds of thousands of dollars. ❞
> MICHAEL BATES

ᴸᴸ I make a very dumb decision at least once a week. **ᴶᴶ**
MICHAEL BATES

HOT TIP: Great books for entrepreneurs and self-employed and independent contractors:

- *Rich Dad, Poor Dad*, by Robert Kiyosaki

- *The Tipping Point*, by Malcolm Gladwell

- *Entrepreneurs Are Made, Not Born* by Lloyd Shetsky

- *Running a One-Person Business* by Claude Whitmyer, Salli Rasberry, and Michael Phillips

- *Making It on Your Own: Surviving and Thriving on the Ups and Downs of Being Your Own Boss* by Paul and Sarah Edwards

- *National Business Employment Weekly Guide to Self-Employment* by David Lord

What business classes did he take during college?

I didn't take a single business course in college. I learned what I know from trial and failure. I fail all the time. The first thing I really botched up was my attempt to buy and sell cars. The first car I bought was a lemon, a bad car. From there I had to learn the mechanics of cars in order to be successful at that business. Getting back to the fact that I didn't take a single business course: I have seen a lot of business professors go through college, do their bachelor's, their master's, and then their Ph.D. and only come out with a lot of textbook business knowledge. But ask them how to build a business from zero cash flow and they wouldn't know how to do it.

After a few years of entrepreneurial ups and downs, Michael figured out how to build a business from basically nothing. He started Software Marketing Corp., (he is now its CEO) at age twenty-six, in an upstairs room of his house, with only $200. By the time Michael was twenty-nine, Software Marketing Corp. was a $12 million company.

Any advice for college students?

I've had at least a five-year plan since the time I was sixteen. I'd think about where I wanted to be a year from now, three years from now, and five years from now. I liked thinking about the big picture rather than the next exam because it made immediate tasks and pressures look like stepping-stones toward my future.

How are you doing in school?

We usually answer that question based on grades. Grades, grades, grades! Their importance has been deeply ingrained in most of us. It seems as if completing your assignments and getting good grades is the urgent bottom line in college. It's easy to feel that good grades are your golden ticket to success. But there is more than one side to this story. Many people don't need good grades in order to be successful.

Before I lay out the reasons why you might not need good grades in order to succeed, let me state the reasons why you might in fact need high marks. First of all, you may have grade requirements imposed on you by outside forces such as financial aid institutions, scholarship funding, club membership, or parental orders. Second, you may desire to attend a graduate school that requires a certain G.P.A. Third, you may just care so much about getting great grades that you can't imagine being able to hold your head up in public without them. If one of these descriptions is you, you'll probably be best served by continuing to make sure your grades are high.

But what if you didn't fall into one of the above situations? What if you're striving for great grades simply because you want to do a good job in school? If this is you, STOP and reconsider, because straight A's will put you at the top of the heap during college, but after college the rules of the game shift dramatically. And if you focus all of your attention on excelling at homework and tests, after graduation you might feel as if you're suited up for football but are stuck in a basketball game. Let me explain.

The vast majority of employers will not ask you about your grades unless they have nothing else to evaluate you by, which is why work experience, internships, and co-op education are so very important. Hard to believe that most employers don't care about your grades? In a recent College Review Board study that asked businesses what they want, employers mentioned ten other things before they mentioned G.P.A. Yes, good grades can help indicate to someone that you are disciplined, but if you believe grades are important outside of academia, you misunderstand how things really work. In academic professions such as teaching, science, or research-oriented work, grades are considered important, but if you're planning to work outside of the college/university environment, you may want to consider what many people have learned: SINCE GRADUATING, NOBODY HAS ASKED ME ABOUT MY G.P.A.

HEY! This chapter isn't about giving you an excuse to get bad grades. It's about giving you logical reasons to allocate your valuable time and energy toward extracurricular activities such as campus clubs, internships, volunteer efforts, or entrepreneurial ventures. From experience, I know that many people don't choose to get involved in these things precisely because they take time and energy away from getting good grades. But hear this: It's a mistake to bet all your money on good grades. Grades aren't everything. In the words of Scott Edelstein, author of *The Truth About College*, "For every successful person who had a high grade point average in college, there's another happy or successful person whose grades were mediocre or unexceptional."

You can always be successful without good grades. But you can't be successful without high self-esteem. Sometimes good grades require such an enormous struggle that your self-esteem and happiness suffer.

> **❝ I drive at night—that's my thinking time. ❞**
> MICHAEL BATES

> **❝ Most people are so busy knocking themselves out trying to do everything they think they should do, they never get around to do what they want to do. ❞**
> KATHLEEN WINSOR, *author*

> **❝ There are two thoughts that will ensure success in all you do: (1) Don't tell everything you know, and (2) until Ace Ventura, no actor had considered talking through his ass. ❞**
> JIM CARREY

HOT TIP: Things that make employers go hmmm . . . key words like

- president
- manager
- editor
- chairperson
- captain
- Phi Beta Kappa

These get recruiters to sit up and take notice.

Source: *Campus Connections* magazine, published by MarketSource Corp.

HOT TIP: Check out the audio program *Better Grades in Less Time,* by Gary Tuerack, at www .totalsuccess.com

Don't let this happen. Instead, shift your focus more toward extracurricular activities. You're likely to feel better about yourself and find areas where you really excel. Consider the testimony of a U.C. Berkeley student who had just won the award for the graduating senior with the highest G.P.A. "In looking back, I'm sad I won it. I could have gotten a 3.5 and still had time to live a normal life. While most other students developed social and leadership skills by joining clubs or other activities, I was busy making sure I didn't get a B on a test."

Don't have regrets when you graduate. The Berkeley student is right in saying that a great G.P.A. is not worth sacrificing enjoyable, important things like social and leadership activities. Especially since the achievement of good grades is often the result of completely absurd circumstances. For instance:

- Susan took U.S. history, thought it was a boring subject, and didn't learn anything she'll remember or use. But Susan was great at memorizing things—like the 50 states and key historical dates—so she got an A in the class.

- In one class, everyone knew that in order to get a good grade, you mostly needed to turn in a paper that was at least 20 pages in length with very few grammatical errors. It didn't really matter what you wrote in it.

- John took algebra and learned more than he'd ever learned before from a class. Unfortunately, because of his obligations to an internship, John did not have time to do all his homework assignments so he got a C.

- A professor did a poor job teaching the subject matter and gave a test nobody was ready for. Paul didn't study an ounce, cheated on the test, and got an A. Karen studied all week, didn't cheat on the test, and got a D.

- Dana took Spanish and learned to speak it well, better than many of the other students. But Dana got an F because he missed more than five classes because of his involvement in a campus club.

- Amy wrote a tremendous paper that demonstrated incredible comprehension of the subject matter, but she had too many grammatical errors so she got a C.

- Jamal learned a lot in his communications course but he clashed with the professor, who didn't seem to like students who had their own opinions. This personality clash resulted in Jamal getting a C instead of a B.

Grades, grades, grades. How can you keep them in proper perspective? Start by remembering Michael Bates's suggestion to focus on the bigger picture and answer the infamous question "How are you doing in school?" with something like, "I'm doing great in school. I'm in a campus club. I'm doing an excellent internship. I'm majoring in a subject that really interests me. I'm developing skills that are going to make

> 66 I always thought the only purpose of going to class was to get an A. I understand now that it's good to get an A, but it's also good to actually get something out of the class. 99
> DEREK CARACCIOLO,
> *communication arts major*

me really valuable to employers. And most of my professors admire me, even if I'm not getting straight A's, because they recognize that I'm learning a lot."

Decide as soon as possible if you're going to work in the fields that require a postgraduate degree, like education or scientific research. If you are going into one of these fields, keep your grades as high as you need to. Often graduate schools require the combination of good grades and extracurricular activities.

If you plan to enter the working world after college, don't sweat your grades so much that they restrict your involvement in extracurriculars. A 3.0 is good. It will keep you in good academic standing and, when coupled with strong extracurricular activities on your resume, will rank as acceptable at many graduate schools if you later choose that route.

If extracurricular activities are having a negative impact on your grades, don't panic. Recognize that racking up time in an extracurricular

> 66 If I could do it over, I would get involved in student activities. That's the best education. 99
> KAREN SOCHER

> 66 The next time you feel the urge to procrastinate . . . just put it off. 99
> UNKNOWN

activity such as an internship, campus club, or a real-world job is usually well worth the difference between getting a B instead of an A. Getting anything below a C is simply shooting yourself in the foot. Doing so puts you on academic probation, and even employers will interpret it as a sign that you can't handle all the responsibilities you take on.

Also, if you're worried about running into an employer who does ask about your grades, remember that this isn't likely to happen if you've got a resume full of extracurriculars and internships. However, if it does happen, you can explain less-than-perfect grades by saying something like: "My G.P.A. was a 3.0, and I'll tell you why it wasn't higher. In addition to learning in the classroom, I felt it important to invest time and energy in extracurricular activities so that my classroom knowledge would be balanced with real-world abilities and skills. So in addition to my studies, I got involved in a campus club and an internship." A smart employer will be impressed.

Finally, remember while you're in college that getting good grades feels like the winning strategy. But in reality, you could complete every assignment, receive straight A's, and still be no closer to a happy life than before you began college. If you don't drive yourself crazy trying for the coveted 4.0, you free up time that can be better used.

Elvis got an F in music

And Nine Other Truths About Grades

- Good grades won't guarantee you happiness, success, or a good job after graduation.

- Grades have very little impact on most students' lives after they leave college.

- If you're going on to graduate school, or to work in academia, your G.P.A. is important.

- If you don't get passing grades, you can't proceed to the next level.

- Grades don't measure intuition, creativity, people skills, or entrepreneurial potential.

- "I got straight A's" is not a good pick-up line.

- Grading isn't solely based on what you learn—often it's based on other things (attendance, personality, paper length, memorization, discrimination, obedience).

- How much you're learning is a better indicator of your future success than your grades.

- Some professors will give you a C when you have learned a lot. Other professors will give you an A when you have learned very little.

- Elvis got an F in music.

Next up: A course-by-course description of the classes that will open doors for you right after college. This is one course catalog you don't want to miss.

HOT TIP: If a class is unrelated to your major, take it pass/no pass. Most colleges let you take up to one-third of your classes pass/no pass, which allows you to explore interesting subjects without worrying about the letter grade. Ask your counselor for more info.

HOT TIP: Check out the website www.how-to-study.com for tons of free studying information.

CHAPTER 11

CLASSES WORTH THEIR WEIGHT IN GOLD

I hated every minute of training, but I said, 'Don't quit. Suffer now and live the rest of your life as a champion.'

MUHAMMAD ALI

HOT TIP: Save the papers that you do in a business-writing course for interview show-and-tell items.

" Academic prose often violates ordinary standards of "good" writing, such as plain language and a conversational tone. At best, this style can be described as formal; at worst, it is jargon-filled, abstract, stilted, and pompous. "
ADAM ROBINSON, *author of* What Smart Students Know *(Crown)*

Not all classes are created equal. Some classes in particular will help you excel in your career. Here are the college courses that are likely to come in handy immediately following your graduation:

Business-Writing Course

Although college may teach you to write academically (usually exploring a subject in depth using an advanced vocabulary), businesses and organizations need you to be able to write papers that are short, simple, and to the point. As a matter of fact, the ability to communicate effectively has been consistently ranked as the number one performance factor for professional success. If you want to look good to your future employers, take a business-writing course. The course usually covers how to write memos, reports, and business letters.

Grant-Writing Course

Being able to get free money to help you do the work of your dreams is a reality if you know how to apply for grants. What is a grant? Let's say you become very rich running a magazine and decide that you want to give $5,000 a year to help other people start magazines. That $5,000 is called a grant and is given to the person with the best application. Now, here's the great part—there are grants for almost everything! In 2004 alone, grants from U.S. foundations totaled $30 billion, and the

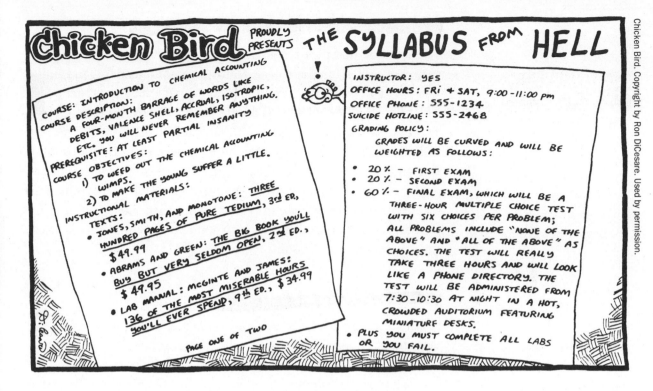

grants were given to assist every purpose under the sun! Once you've completed a grant-writing course, you'll know how to find and apply for the grant money. Knowing how to apply for grant money is a valuable skill that many businesses need and pay money for. When I was at Levi Strauss & Co., somebody just out of college got hired specifically for their grant-writing skills. Levi Strauss, like many large companies, has a department that gives away grant money. In addition, a grant-writing course might be your key to having the money you need to do the work of your dreams.

HOT TIP: To find grant information, ask a librarian for directories on foundation funding, or check out http://fdncenter.org.

Promotions/Public Relations Course

Take a course that covers paid and unpaid activities designed to encourage the purchase of products and services including advertising, display, publicity/press releases, public relations, packaging, special events, and sale promotions. I encourage you to take a public relations course because you'll find that all companies can benefit from good public relations. Taking this course could open up a lot of job opportunities for you.

❝ Success isn't magic, but then magic isn't magic either. ❞
UNKNOWN

Speech/Business Presentations Course

Take a course that includes discussions and practice on delivering persuasive speeches, body language, assertive communications, and audiovisual aids. I've said it before and it's important enough to repeat: THE ABILITY TO COMMUNICATE EFFECTIVELY HAS BEEN CONSISTENTLY RANKED THE NUMBER ONE PERFORMANCE FACTOR FOR PROFESSIONAL SUCCESS. In our society, shyness is not considered an asset. A speech course can help you feel confident speaking to one or one thousand. And you can apply this confidence to situations that occur more often than in public speaking: speaking well over the phone; speaking up in class; making a good impression in an interview; and expressing your ideas in a meeting.

HOT TIP: The best way to improve your communication skills is by practice, and the best organization to practice in is Toastmasters. Check out www.toastmasters.org to find a club near you.

Sales/Selling Principles Course

Sales courses are helpful to everyone no matter what their professional aspirations. A good sales course will cover customer service, the processes and techniques of selling, time and activity planning, product/service knowledge, supporting activities, and managing the selling function. In addition to being a valuable skill in every field, knowing how to sell yourself is the key to winning the jobs and salaries you desire. Studies suggest that you're going to need to win at least ten different jobs during your lifetime. So remember, if you can't sell yourself or your ideas, nobody will buy your services.

HOT TIP: There are student centers on the Web. They are loaded with resume examples, cover letter samples, personality tests, and career advisors. You need to check them out. Start with a couple I like: www.collegegrad.com and www.focusedstudent.com.

Time Management Workshop

Time management is a great tool everyone can use to work more effectively. You need to develop a system that allows you to get the most done in the least time. It's a wonder that it's not a required course for college students, because it's practically a required skill in the real world.

Internship Course

Most colleges offer classes that help you find great internships. You get class credit for getting out of the classroom and experiencing what different jobs are really like . . . what a good deal! You also get the support of your instructor to handle unforeseen workplace challenges you get to network with other students, who also have great internships and could easily open up new doors for you; and it is a great introduction to use when you call companies looking for an internship.

Human Relations/Interpersonal Communications Course

Master the ability to get along well with almost anybody in everyday business and social situations. Develop the ability even if you have to learn it on your own. Your college might not offer a course to help you develop your "people skills," but if it does, the course is probably called "Human Relations" (as in "I can relate to humans") or "Interpersonal Communications." A good course promotes understanding of oneself and empathy for others as a basis for establishing satisfactory relationships on the job and in everyday living. It also covers listening skills and group decision-making processes. If your college offers such a course, take it—maybe even twice.

HOT TIP: On the Internet, www.daytimer .com has some free time management resources.

HOT TIP: Resolve to speak up once in every class. This habit alone will make you a good communicator.

Marketing Course

Every business has a marketing plan. Artists who make a living selling their art have to use marketing principles. Performers and athletes market themselves like products. Colleges are marketed to high school students and parents. Churches have fundraising drives that are based on marketing. NBA basketball teams are marketed to the public. Everywhere you go in your work, marketing will be a part of the picture. If you take a marketing course, you'll have a fundamental understanding of a subject that everyone will be involved in at some time. It also looks great on your resume. Most courses will cover marketing environment, segmentation, marketing mix, marketing opportunities, and buyer behavior.

HOT TIP: Read Joe Girard's *How to Sell Yourself* (Warner Books).

Language Course

Many major companies are doing business globally and they look for employees who can speak another language—or who have taken language classes. It shows an interest and ability to learn new languages. Even if you'll only work in the United States, learn a second language. Research trends point to a very near future when speaking a second language will be a necessary skill.

Take the courses described above and you'll have more than an interesting library in your head on the day you graduate. You'll have the business basics that most employers require. Best of all, you'll have the know-how that will enable you to accomplish your dreams.

HOT TIP: Don't leave college without knowing how to use Microsoft Word, Excel, Access, and PowerPoint.

Making College Work for You

As you may already know from firsthand experience, the way a school teaches may not always be the best way for you to learn. For some, college is an easy way to learn because it matches their learning style. But for many others, listening and reading are terribly difficult ways to learn—like trying to eat rice with a toothpick.

Learning-style specialist Renee Mollan-Masters, author of the book *You Are Smarter Than You Think!*, put it this way:

Inside I knew I was smart, but I was never able to perform well in school. In high school, I would study the same way my friends were studying except that I would put in considerably more hours and they would get the A's and I would get the C's. This seemed unfair and confusing because, after all, I had put in more time. Learning changed for me when I began studying speech pathology. I was learning almost instantly. I graduated with honors. Even years later I was still unaware of what had caused this sudden change in my intellectual ability.

Renee soon realized what made all the difference—for her to really learn something, not just memorize it for a short while, she had to discover and rely on her particular learning strengths. Listening to a lecture wasn't enough.

I recommend that you read Renee's book and determine *your* personal learning style. Next you'll learn how to explode your success rate in college by mastering your life one minute at a time.

HOT TIP: Over enroll at class registration and then drop the classes with professors you don't like.

❝ According to the latest official figures, 43.28 percent of all statistics are totally useless. ❞
MIKE WATERS

CHAPTER 12

SUCCESS ON YOUR TIME

Don't say you don't have enough time. You have exactly the same number of hours per day that were given to Helen Keller, Pasteur, Michelangelo, Mother Teresa, Leonardo da Vinci, Thomas Jefferson, and Albert Einstein.

H. JACKSON BROWN, JR., author

A very revealing research study on college students is detailed in the book *Making the Most of College* by Harvard professor Richard Light. In the book, the author tells how over the course of twenty years he interviewed college students at Harvard in person about their college experience. And what he found was that the most successful students always mentioned a particular concept during their interviews. It was a concept that unsuccessful students almost never mentioned no matter how long he spoke to them. The concept was "time management."

Let me confess, I had never even HEARD about time management in college. But I've learned a lot about it since. It is in the top five of my greatest success tools.

Effective time management is one of the key separating factors between those who achieve their dreams and those who look back on their lives overwhelmed with regret. In the simplest terms, time management is the ability to effectively organize your time and responsibilities in order to get the most out of your day. It is important to note that "the most out of your day" is subjective. In other words, you get to decide what this means for you. Once you realize that, time management becomes a game. How can you more effectively organize your time to get the biggest bang for your buck? Your life is an untold story, and you hold the pen. You get to decide what you spend your time doing and what opportunities you let pass by. If going out to dinner with your friends

> Someday, you may be lucky enough to achieve the status of 'elder statesman.' People will come to the mountaintop and they'll listen to you. For now, spend some time applying the best principles of P. T. Barnum and Dale Carnegie down here on the flatlands. Become good at the art of explaining and defending your ideas.
> WIN BORDEN

is a top priority, then manage your time to allow you to do that. This doesn't mean studying less, it means organizing your day to study at a different time so your evening is free. As I said, you hold the pen.

How to get started with time management

Here is the really good news: all time management skills are learned. The first step is to become aware of what you spend your time doing. Then you can study a number of techniques to help you increase your effectiveness. Read over the following ideas and see which time management tools would be helpful in your life.

Focusing on Your Priorities

No matter what your hobbies, interests, or career aspirations, good time management skills can help you do more, better, faster, and easier. However, learning these skills is pointless unless you are sure you are using them to get meaningful results. For example, if you don't really like TV and just watch a few hours here and there to pass time, becoming more effective with your time so you can watch more TV is kind of missing the point. Look back over the first section of this book, which helped you discover and take action on your true passions, then study and use time management tools to work more effectively toward your goals.

The following excerpt is from one of my favorite books on time management, titled *First Things First,* by Steven R. Covey, A. Roger Merrill, and Rebecca R. Merrill. It is a great metaphor for effective time management.

I attended a seminar once where the instructor was lecturing on time. At one point, he said, "Okay, it's time for a quiz." He reached under the table and pulled out a wide-mouth gallon jar. He set it on the table next to a platter with some fist-sized rocks on it. "How many of these rocks do you think we can get in the jar?" he asked.

After we made our guess, he said, "Okay, let's find out." He set one rock in the jar . . . then another . . . then another. I don't remember how many he got in, but he got the jar full. Then he asked, "Is the jar full?"

Everybody looked at the rocks and said, "Yes."

> **"** The bad news is time flies. The good news is you're the pilot. **"**
> MICHAEL ALTSHULER,
> *leadership coach*

> **"** A wise person does at once what a fool does at last. Both do the same thing, only at different times. **"**
> BALTASAR GRACIAN,
> *philosopher*

The he said, "Ahh." He reached under the table and pulled out a bucket of gravel. Then he dumped some gravel in and shook the jar and the gravel went in all the little spaces left by the big rocks. Then he grinned and said once more, "Is the jar full?"

By this time we were on to him. "Probably not," we said.

"Good!" he replied. And he reached under the table and brought out a bucket of sand. He started dumping the sand in and it went in all the little spaces left by the rocks and gravel. Once more he looked at us and said, "Is the jar full?"

"No!" we all roared.

He said, "Good!" and he grabbed a pitcher of water and began to pour it in. He got something like a quart of water in that jar. Then he said, "Well, what's the point?"

Somebody said, "There are gaps and if you really work at it, you can always fit more into your life."

"No," he said, "that's not the point. The point is this: If you hadn't put these big rocks in first, you would never have gotten any of them in."

What are the big rocks in your life? Family, friends, health, school . . . make sure you are putting these big rocks in first. Once you get these taken care of, then you can worry about the gravel, sand, and last, the water.

Dealing with Stress

Don't let stress stress you out. Good time management skills can help you arrange your time better so you can handle the inevitable stresses of life. Finals coming up in a few weeks? Sit down today and start organizing your priorities to ensure that when the big exams roll around, you are ready for them without pushing through all-nighters and pulling out your hair.

ℴ Many people seem to think that success in one area can compensate for failure in other areas. But can it really? . . . True effectiveness requires balance. ⫸
STEPHEN COVEY, *author*

Get Organized and Save Time

There are a lot of great software programs that enable you to get organized, save time, and accomplish more. These programs have great "to do" list capabilities (finally, you don't have to keep rewriting a new list every day). They also have calendar functions so that you can organize your schedule. They offer effective ways to organize all those important bits of information that normally get lost on a scrap of paper. Check out websites such as http://effexis.com and http://vip-qualitysoft.com for example programs, or simpler (and free) versions such as Yahoo! and Google Calendar.

Beat Procrastination

One of the most challenging aspects of time management is procrastination. It is essential for you to identify the causes of procrastination and start fighting them right away. One common technique used to help prevent procrastination is breaking up your work into small and easily achievable projects. For example, instead of thinking that you need to sit down and write your entire paper this afternoon, just decide to give it one hour with the goal of finding your first two site references. The main thing is to get the ball rolling. Most likely, once you start you will realize that the project isn't as big as you made it out to be in your head.

Another technique to beat procrastination is to set deadlines in advance of the real deadline. Call a friend or a parent and tell them you are going to have the first two pages of your big report done by this Friday. When you publicly commit to doing something, you become much more motivated to get your butt off the couch and start working. Use this technique and you will find that by the time the real deadline comes around, you will be as relaxed as you are on summer vacation because your project was done days ago.

Take the Time to Make the Time

The point of this chapter is to give you a general understanding of the importance of time management. The brief techniques described above should serve as food for thought, but to really increase your effectiveness you will need to learn how to implement additional tools. There are a number of great books full of time management tips. As I mentioned

> " To think too long about doing a thing often becomes its undoing. "
> EVA YOUNG

> " A year from now you will wish you had started today. "
> KAREN LAMB, *author*

> " The surest way to be late is to have plenty of time. "
> LEO KENNEDY, *author*

> **❝ One worthwhile task carried to a successful conclusion is worth half-a-hundred half-finished tasks. ❞**
> MALCOLM S. FORBES, *former publisher of* Forbes *magazine*

above, *First Things First* by Stephen Covey is a great book, but it's just the tip of the iceberg. Check out www.amazon.com, and type in "time management" in the search box, then see what books seem the most helpful.

Time management is an essential characteristic in the ability to major in success. In the next chapter, you will read about a student who chose to spend his time at university gaining an exceptional leadership experience and making a positive impact on hundreds of other students.

CHAPTER 13

EXCEL-ERATION TRAINING

Leaders grow; they are not made.

PETER F. DRUCKER FOUNDATION

Leadership training is consistently ranked as one of the top qualities that employers are looking for in job candidates, but what does "leadership training" really mean and how do you get it? Well, the best way is to put yourself in a leadership position and learn from real-life experience. Every campus has opportunities for students to take on leadership roles. Find something you are interested in and volunteer for a leadership position.

Anton Anderson's story is a great example of valuable leadership experience one can gain while still in school. In his senior year, Anton started a chapter of a national organization called The National Society of Leadership and Success.

The first time I heard about The National Society of Leadership and Success was at a college summer camp called Eagle University. Gary Tuerack, the president of the society, told us about the organization and its unique approach to university success. Within thirty minutes his vision and energy had completely changed my philosophy on college.

The more I researched the society, the more excited I became. I quickly decided to start a chapter at my school (University of California, Santa Barbara), but to my surprise the idea initially received negative feedback. Numerous faculty members, students, and professors told me that "an organization like this wouldn't work at our university, and besides, it was nothing new, we already had 298 clubs on campus and students didn't need or want another one."

> Leadership is not so much about technique and methods as it is about opening the heart. Leadership is about inspiration—of oneself and of others. Great leadership is about human experiences, not processes. Leadership is not a formula or a program, it is a human activity that comes from the heart and considers the hearts of others.
>
> LANCE SECRETAN,
> *leadership coach*

❝ I learned early on that it really isn't a big deal if one door shuts in your face. Just brush off your shoulders and go knock on the next door. ❞
ANTON ANDERSON

❝ Always give credit where credit is due. My biggest regret is not giving enough credit to my adviser. None of it would have been possible without her and unfortunately, I don't know if the members realized the extent of her work. ❞
ANTON ANDERSON

❝ As a leader, it is your job to get others involved. The more others are involved, the more invested they will become in the group's mission and goals. ❞
ANTON ANDERSON

This was the first major roadblock Anton faced, and although these responses discouraged him, he stuck to his goal.

I kept at it and eventually found a great adviser named Britt Andreatta who was in charge of leadership development at the university. She was incredible! Having the right mentor is invaluable. Step one was done, now all I had to do was find three students interested in being officers and I would be able to begin the official process of becoming a certified chapter. Unfortunately, I was met yet again with an unfavorable surprise; most students were suspicious of new organizations and already felt overloaded with work. I quickly realized this was a matter of my approach, so I eased off and headed back to the drawing board. I had several meetings with Britt behind the scenes and learned everything I could from Gary Tuerack and Angela Schutz, the national president and chapter mentor of the society. Finally, after two months of planning, we began our membership drive.

I remember very clearly the day the membership invitation letters were sent out, thinking, "OK, I just need three members, come on." The following morning I eagerly checked my email and was ecstatic to see that exactly three members had joined! I ran out of my room and yelled, "Hey, you will never believe it, I have three members. We are going to form a chapter!" To my surprise, the emails didn't stop at three. The next day twelve members joined, followed by forty-six, then seventy-three . . . and it continued like this. Close to six hundred members joined by the first day of school.

Up to this point, Anton's experience was unique and exciting, but the true leadership training started the first week of school.

I quickly organized an introduction meeting and rented the second largest room on campus. The event was scheduled for 6 PM, and I arrived two hours early to set up. You can imagine my surprise when I opened the doors for the first time and was greeted by what felt like a thousand students, all standing anxiously in a line which weaved down the street and around the corner, ending just short of our off-campus pizza shop. This was one of the highlights of my life. I welcomed all 550 students who attended that evening with a well-rehearsed speech sharing my genuine appreciation and excitement for the upcoming journey we were embarking on together. The students responded with a moti-

vated applause, followed by eager questions regarding the possibility of others joining. I will never forget the way I felt going to sleep that night. My goal of bringing the resources offered by the society to my campus was being realized. And even more exhilarating was the fact that I knew it was just the beginning!

At the meeting, I shared details about officer positions and encouraged people to apply. I was extremely fortunate to have a number of outstanding applicants and within one week we formed an extraordinary officer board. Over the year, we grew our organization to over 1,100 members! At the time, it was three times larger than any other student-led association at my university and almost two times the size of any other chapter across the nation.

What were some of the biggest benefits Anton gained from his leadership experience?

There were two different types of benefits from my work: the tangible and intangible. On the tangible side of the coin, I received numerous scholarships and awards, including the University Service Award for my positive impact on the campus, the UCSB Student Leader of the Year with the Excellence in Leadership Award, and the National Society Student President of the Year.

On the intangible side of the coin, and much more significant to me, is the knowledge that my leadership activities made a positive impact on others' lives. Throughout the year, I received countless letters from students sharing the dramatic impact the society had on their lives, the excitement and passion they discovered inside of themselves, and the good deeds they are continually doing.

Looking back on the experience, what do you think Anton is the most proud of?

I was honored by the awards, but the thing I am most proud of today is the present strength of the chapter. Upon my graduation, I left the organization in the hands of a few amazing student leaders and they have taken the chapter to a new level. It promises to be a strong organization for years to come and has forever made its mark on the university campus.

❝ The only test of leadership is that somebody follows. **❞**
ROBERT K. GREENLEAF,
leadership philosopher

❝ One of the biggest lessons I learned is the importance of asking for help. At first, I tried to do everything myself, but I quickly realized it was too much for one person. Never be ashamed to ask others for help. **❞**
ANTON ANDERSON

❝ A study at Cornell University's Johnson Graduate School of Management found that compassion and building teamwork will be two of the most important charactcristics business leaders will need for success a decade from now. **❞**
DOC CHILDRE AND BRUCE CRYER,
the founder and the CEO of HeartMath training group

HOT TIP: If starting
your own leadership
program sounds interesting
to you, check out the
National Society of
Leadership and Success
(http://societyofsuccess.
com). There may be a
chapter of the NSLS on
your campus already for
you to join and benefit
from. Check their website!

HOT TIP: Check out
www.asgaonline.com for
leadership conferences
and their publication,
Student Leader magazine.
Also check out http://
ncslcollege.com (National
Conference on Student
Leadership) and http://
nslcleaders.org (National
Student Leadership
Conference) to learn about
opportunities to attend
conferences on student
leadership.

Some students attend conferences. Some organize the conferences themselves. Some read books. Some participate in "ropes courses" and find themselves perched high in a tree, trying to find the courage to walk a wire tightrope fifty feet above the ground. Although their activities are vastly different, they are all getting leadership training.

In my work as a speaker, I've come to learn that there are a fortunate few students, like the ones in the examples, who are gaining a huge advantage during college by learning exciting, out-of-the-ordinary lessons. Somehow they tap into an entire body of knowledge that isn't mentioned in the typical college education—knowledge about being effective!

Effectiveness is simply the ability to make something happen. Leaders are usually effective people. Test your effectiveness knowledge by asking yourself if you can do the following things with confidence:

- formulate a team vision

- run an effective meeting

- get the cooperation of many different people

- organize a staff for effective action

- assess the varying needs of diverse team members

- plan a large activity from start to finish

- delegate effectively

- publicize your cause

- overcome declining morale

- speak publicly

- think through difficult problems

- evaluate risks and make important decisions

If you haven't had experience in the skills above you're not alone—but you are at a disadvantage because some students are gaining a competitive edge by learning the secrets to being effective. Let me explain. College most likely is not going to teach you these skills, and the vast majority of students are going to graduate without being able to do them well. But what if you knew how to gain this expertise on your own?

The ART OF THE STAMPEDE

"You see, I was right! We were supposed to all be running in the same direction."

What businesses want:

1. Leadership ability
2. Computer proficiency
3. Exceptional people skills
4. Oral and written communications skills
5. A demonstrated team attitude
6. Flexibility
7. Problem-solving skills and decision-making abilities
8. Curiosity
9. Energy
10. Knowledge of other cultures and languages

Source: College Review Board

Gain the advantage

If you want the best from your college experience, go straight to the student life office or the counseling center and ask about leadership programs. If your college offers a leadership program, find a way to join it! These programs are an unbelievably great experience, from the things you learn to the way they teach the lessons. Often these programs are conducted on rope courses or wilderness retreats—fun and challenging stuff!

If by some strange luck of the draw there is no leadership program at your school, or if you don't particularly connect with the one that does exist, there is no need to stress . . . start your own! It will be one of the best experiences of your college career and is much easier than it may sound. It will allow you to meet tons of ambitious students such as yourself, network with the movers and shakers on your campus, give you incredibly valuable experience, and it looks great on your resume!

> **❝** They always say that time changes things, but you actually have to change them yourself. **❞**
> ANDY WARHOL, *artist*

> **❝** Use what talents you possess: The woods would be very silent if no birds sang there except those that sang best. **❞**
> HENRY VAN DYKE, *author and clergyman*

Plus, the biggest benefit is that if you do it right it will still be going strong after you graduate. You will leave your mark on your campus for years to come.

Next, pick up a course catalog and start looking for courses that cover topics like:

- planning
- decision making
- leadership
- human relations
- problem solving
- personal development
- time management

My favorite leadership books:

- *How to Win Friends and Influence People* by Dale Carnegie (Pocket Books)
- *Awaken the Giant Within* by Anthony Robbins (Simon and Schuster)
- *Finding Your Purpose* by Barbara Braham (Crisp Publications)
- *Life 101* by John-Roger and Peter McWilliams (Bantam Books)
- *Six Action Shoes* by Edward de Bono (Penguin Books)
- *Sacred Hoops* by Phil Jackson (Hyperion Books)
- *Leading Out Loud: The Authentic Speaker, the Credible Leader* by Terry Pearce (Jossey-Bass)
- *The Pursuit of Wow* by Tom Peters (Vintage Books)
- *Handbook for the Positive Revolution* by Edward de Bono (Viking Penguin)

These aren't traditional courses and often are offered by a special department (for example, counseling centers, career centers, or extended education courses for returning students). These are courses in effectiveness. They teach you exciting lessons that you can use in your everyday life. (Did I mention that taking them also impresses future employers?)

Last but not least, ask at the career center for the best place on campus to find personal achievement books, CDs, and DVDs. It's exciting and surprising to find that at almost every college I visit many of the books that changed my life are available for students to check out. Usually these books and media are located in the career center, the student activities office, the counseling center, or the main library.

Don't blow off leadership courses!

"Leadership ability" was the number one quality named as "what businesses want" in a survey by the College Review Board. The resources I've recommended will not only increase your productivity after college, they'll save you money. People pay big bucks to learn these lessons ($3,000 is not an unusual amount for a three-day seminar on leadership or personal achievement).

Philosophically speaking

Most students are going to pride themselves on being intelligent or talented. But beware of priding yourself on these things because, in the words of Calvin Coolidge, "Nothing is more common than unsuccessful people with talent. Unrewarded genius is almost a proverb." Instead, take pride in being able to "make it happen."

The lessons you learn from the activities suggested in this chapter do teach you to excel. Take these lessons, then use them to get in the fast lane to success by learning from a pro.

HOT TIP: Campus clubs are often organized in the following categories: associated students, academic/honorary, career, community service, cultural, ethnic, fraternities/sororities, ideological, political, recreational, religious, residence halls, and special interest. Any categories look interesting?

CHAPTER 14

A MAJOR SHORTCUT

Alone we can do so little; together we can do so much.

HELEN KELLER

If you want to excel at something—maybe it's a game, a sport, or a career—there is one method for becoming great that beats all others. The fastest way to excel at something is to BE COACHED BY THE BEST! Because:

- Successful people can tell you the shortcuts.

- People who have mastered the game can teach you key strategies and moves.

- Successful people can open doors for you by introducing you to other successful (and important) people and resources.

- Being around a person who's really good at his/her job provides you with a crystal-clear picture of the habits and traits you'll need.

- A good coach can give you specific advice about your individual strengths and weaknesses.

- Even your passion and enthusiasm will be strengthened simply by being around someone who lives passionately and enthusiastically.

In short, being around someone who's doing or has done things that you admire is fantastically inspiring and incredibly revealing. Asking for help is a key ingredient in winning a "success coach." My first success coach was Deborah Lowe, a professor at San Francisco State University.

44 Do not be content merely to recognize greatness in others; take a further step and imitate it. For in the imitation of greatness is greatness itself. **77**
SHERMAN FINESILVER, *chief judge, U.S. District Court, commencement address*

44 Somehow figure out a way to meet the top individuals in your ideal industry and do anything and everything possible to learn from them. **77**
ANTON ANDERSON

I was enrolled in one of Deborah Lowe's classes and, in no time at all, her knowledge and accomplishments impressed me. One day after class I asked her for help on a cover letter I was trying to write. During the process of getting her help, I also won her respect and her willingness to help me reach my career ambitions. For the next two years, I learned what it feels like to have a success coach. (It feels like you've got a top expert on your side.)

In addition to the encouragement and inspiration that cannot be measured, my success coach taught me many things I never learned in class. She pounded the importance of internships into my thick and reluctant head. She taught me how to write an outstanding resume. She showed me where to look for work and how to get paid as much as possible. She taught me how to "package" myself to win whatever job I desired. And on and on. But the one thing I got from her which is perhaps the most difficult benefit to describe is simply that being around a great person rubs off. Without even trying, somehow I'm a little more like the Deborah Lowe I admire so much.

A success coach is . . .

A success coach is anyone who takes the time to teach you about succeeding. Often the coaching process is called "mentoring." But whether you choose to call this person a "mentor" or a "coach," you're looking for someone who has accomplished things that you'd like to accomplish and is kind enough and willing to take time each week to help you.

The key to getting a coach

The key to getting a coach is a three-letter word: ASK. Ask the right person, ask for help, ask with conviction, ask until you get what you want. A good place to start is with your parents and friends. Explain to them what you are interested in learning more about and ask them if they know anyone in that line of work who may be able to help you. You will be amazed with the connections you had and didn't even realize! If you ask, you'll receive.

Maybe your success coach is one of your professors. Have you had a professor that you really admired? Maybe it's a professor that you haven't met yet. Ask your friends for recommendations. Maybe it's a staff member in the career center or the student development center, or

HOT TIP: Ask your success coach to write you a letter of recommendation when you're applying for a job. And when you ask, dress professionally. You want your letter written with that image in mind.

❝ The first thing is to realize that you cannot achieve ultimate success alone. Luckily, I was able to get the best coach there is, Tom Telez. I couldn't coach myself. So look for the best coach there is. ❞
CARL LEWIS, *winner of nine Olympic gold medals*

someone you admire where you work. Maybe it's someone you know who's already in the working world or one of your peers who seems to be really advanced.

Try these ideas:

- Find someone you admire and ask them for help with your career development.

- Try to become their assistant or helper; make it clear that all you want is to learn from their experiences.

- Invite them to be a guest lecturer in your campus club.

Convincing a success coach that you're worthy

As a rule, you have to win a person's respect before they will coach you. There are exceptions to this rule: Career center counselors and student development staff are paid to coach any student who asks, and they offer self-help books, which can either be purchased or read on loan. But in cases where the person is not obligated to coach you, you need to make a good impression. How do you do this? It's hard to say no to someone who demonstrates the following qualities:

- admiration, demonstrated by asking for help, complimenting their expertise, and being grateful for their advice

- ambition, demonstrated by expressing your goals and dreams

- follow-through, demonstrated by taking their advice and completing what you said you would

- courtesy, demonstrated by being considerate of their time and by being well mannered

- respect, demonstrated by trusting what they say

Stay worthy

Being "coached" is not always an easy process. To help you succeed, coaches often have to point out your weaknesses or push you to expand your thinking. Rarely are we taught how to take criticism and even if

> **" In the long run, it is much more valuable to spend your time seeking information from the experts than seeking immediate money. "**
> ANTON ANDERSON

> **" All glory comes from daring to begin. "**
> EUGENE WARE, *lawyer and poet*

> **" I had a lot of mentors. I would go to poetry readings looking for a writing mentor and instead of bombarding them with questions I would hand them a prewritten letter that they could read on their way home. "**
> VERONICA CHAMBERS, *story editor for* New York Times Magazine

we can, it remains a painful process. This story may help you work well with your coach.

A Zen master was once asked by a professor (who was widely known for his book learning) to explain Zen to him. The master agreed and began by pouring him a cup of tea. But once the cup was full, the master kept pouring and the tea overflowed into a puddle. "Enough!" said the professor. "The cup is already full and now it is overflowing." "Your mind," said the Zen master, "is like this cup—so filled with your own ideas, views, and concepts that there is no room for any new learning."

Rarely will people coach someone who is resistant to suggestions. Suggestions are hard to take because they can make you feel embarrassed, but suggestions are also your fast pass to growth. When being coached, bite your tongue, put your own views and opinions aside, and try out the suggestions of your coach. If after giving them your best try, you decide that the suggestions are not for you, then you can revert to what you believe is best.

Take the shortcut

Now that you know the fastest way to excel at anything, I'm going to tell you about a simple and exciting activity that can change your life in an instant.

66 I do not think much of a man who is not wiser today than he was yesterday. 99
ABRAHAM LINCOLN

66 I think the success came because in my heart I was still always that young kid from Elmira, hustling for work and for something better, and because I always surrounded myself with great people. 99
TOMMY HILFIGER

CHAPTER 15

LIFE-CHANGING REALITY CHECKS

The journey of 10,000 miles begins with a single phone call.
CONFUCIUS BELL

his life was opened up due to networking

> ❝ Learn to call strangers fearlessly and you gain one more key to success. ❞
> DONALD ASHER, *author of* From College to Career: Entry-Level Resumes for Any Major *(Ten Speed Press)*

HOT TIP: According to research about networking, you are only six acquaintances away from a personal connection to anyone in the world. Six calls away from the most incredible informational interview you can imagine! Go for it.

One day, somebody suggested to San Francisco State student David Greene that "informational interviewing" might be a way to discover a good career. After it was explained to David that informational interviewing was just a friendly way to ask a professional some job questions, he called and spoke with a woman at IBM. He had gotten the name of the woman through a friend of a friend. His informational interview at IBM went great. Even though he didn't apply for work, IBM said there might be the possibility of an internship! The woman also told him about a small company named Interactive Records that puts music and multimedia together. That sounded like a dream job, so he called them. Right away they said, "We're not hiring." David replied, "I'm not calling to ask for a job. I am calling because I heard that you are doing cutting-edge work, and I'd just like to learn more about it." He said the right thing and Interactive Records said, "Oh! Well, why don't you come next week and we'll show you around." David went on this informational interview and basically never left. He's now part owner in the company.

You want your dream job to come true faster? Or perhaps still not 100 percent sure what your dream job is? Info-interview with someone who has a job you would love to have. David Greene feels that one informational interview changed his life. It took him from no job to his dream job! During speeches, I ask who in the audience has done an informational interview. A few hands usually go up. The people who have done them usually say one of three things:

"It was great. I learned a lot about the job and about how to get into the field."

"It was great and they offered me a job!"

"I'm glad I did it because I discovered that it's not my dream job after all!"

Informational interviews provide you with two great things: Answers and connections. In person or over the phone, you interview someone about their job: "What is the job really like? How much does it pay? How do people get into this field?" That's basically all there is to informational interviewing. You talk to a working professional and you get "real-world" insights into the job that interests you. Imagine whom you could interview if you really aimed high.

HOT TIP: Always send a thank you letter within one week and let them know if you have, or plan to, act on their advice.

Nuts and bolts of informational interviewing

Any time you are interested in a profession, call someone working in the profession, tell them you are a student, and ask them if you can come in for an informational interview. There's no one in the world you can't try contacting. People like to help students out with job information. I know one student whose dream job was to run a Fortune 500 company, so he called the president of Levi Strauss & Co., asked for an informational interview, and got it!

To find a working professional, go to your college career center or alumni office and ask for a list of people who are working in the field that interests you. Locate alumni, people you've read about, or people your parents know. Then call those people and say something like:

HOT TIP: You may have to contact the company/ individual multiple times before they agree to set an appointment with you. Don't take it personally and keep pursuing, it is just part of the process.

> *Hi, my name is _____ and I'm a student at _____.*
> *I got your name from _____. You're in a line of work that I'm interested in and I was hoping that you could help me gain insights into the profession. I'm sure that my questions could be answered in a ten-to fifteen-minute informational interview.*

Most of the time they will be more than willing to take ten to fifteen minutes to answer your questions. Sometimes they will want to talk over the phone, but often they will invite you to their workplace. When you can, choose that the interview be at their workplace because you'll learn more and make a stronger connection with the person.

Great questions to ask during the interview:

- How did you get into this field?

- What do you do on a daily basis?

HOT TIP: Newspapers are a good source for learning about jobs but not in the help wanted ads. Write to people you read about, congratulate them, and ask them for an informational interview.

HOT TIP: Go to career fairs put on by your college. Get information about job opportunities and ask questions. Even if you aren't interested in working for the company, pay attention to the key things they are looking for. This gives you great insight into the minds of the employers.

HOT TIP: College librarians often have access to online subscription services like Dow-Jones Interactive and the Standard & Poor's Industry Surveys. Two great ways to get high-dollar information about companies for FREE!

ff It takes seven attempts to make an unsolicited business contact. Most people give up after three. **"**
DON ASHER, *author of* The Overnight Job Change Strategy *(Ten Speed Press)*

- What percentage of your time is spent doing what?

- What are the skills that are most important for a position in this field?

- What were the keys to your career advancement?

- Why did you decide to work for this company?

- What do you like most about this company?

- How does your company differ from its competitors?

- What do you like and not like about working in this industry?

- How is the economy affecting this industry?

- What are the professional associations related to this industry?

- What would you do differently if you had it to do over?

And most importantly . . .

- What advice would you give to me that I can apply now?

After you ask each question, it is crucial that you just listen. Don't talk, don't interrupt, give them time to fully answer the question. If they pause but they look as if they have more on their mind, ask "Is there anything else?" and then sit and listen again. This is like tapping into a gold mine of wealth. Things that took them years to learn (not to mention a lot of money) you are going to learn in an hour!

One Caution

Don't mix informational interviewing with job seeking. Employers will grant informational interviews when they firmly trust that you will not hit them up for a job. The minute you begin trying to get a job, the employer is going to feel misled. If you discover a job that you do want to apply for during the interview, wait until the informational interview is over. The next day, call the employer and tell them that the informational interview not only confirmed your interest in the field but also made you aware of a position you would like to formally apply for.

Sometimes they may offer you an internship or job. Many people have conducted informational interviews and have done nothing but ask questions and yet have been offered employment. What do you do if they offer you an internship or job? If it sounds good, take it! Your life changes in an instant!

Go forth and investigate!

Now you know how to get the inside scoop on your dream job. Info-interviewing can lead to your dream job or connect you to a mentor, because employers are very impressed by students who have the savvy to do it. There's something else that really impresses employers. It's revealed on the next page.

HOT TIP: Read magazines that cover the field you're interested in and call someone who was profiled. Mention that you read the article and were very impressed. This is nice flattery.

CHAPTER 16

REALLY GET INTO IT

Success is not the result of spontaneous combustion. You must set yourself on fire.

REGGIE LEACH, professional ice hockey player

Veronica Chambers has loved reading books ever since she was a kid. But because she thought you had to be anointed or chosen to be a writer, her sophomore year at Simon's Rock College was spent pursuing a legal career. Veronica was working at a legal firm and taking prelaw classes until she noticed that a friend of hers who was interning at a magazine "was definitely having a much better time than I was."

Then the question quickly arose: How could she get a similar internship?

It was really hard. I was a sophomore. I didn't have any journalism experience. I hadn't even taken a journalism class! All I could think to do was sit down with the telephone book and call every magazine in New York. "No, no, no, no," was all I heard until I got to the S's and Sassy magazine. They had just started up and they said, "If you want to work for free, come on down."

> **"** Try your idea and if it doesn't work, come up with the next one. Keep trying and keep trying and eventually something works. **"**
> VERONICA CHAMBERS, *interned with* Sassy *magazine*

The internship at *Sassy* magazine opened doors for Veronica to do summer and winter internships at the magazines *Seventeen*, *Life*, and *Essence*. On her second internship at *Seventeen* magazine she wanted to write, but they required previously published articles. She talked a local high school newspaper into letting her write a few entertainment stories.

You were supposed to be a high schooler to write for the paper but they let me do it after I pointed out that I was only one year older than some of the seniors. When the articles came out, I showed them to the editor of Seventeen *and I begged them to let me write. They started me off with tiny assignments but when I saw my first nationally published article I was so psyched, I instantly started a scrapbook!*

Within a short time, Veronica found herself getting assignments to interview celebrities. She remembers her roommates being excited every time they'd take messages "from famous people they thought were very cool." When she got her own monthly column in *Seventeen* magazine, she was still a junior and had yet to take a journalism class. "It was a tiny column called 'Guy Talk,' nothing big, but it was fun and I got paid $250 each month."

Veronica enjoyed a lot of great internship experiences during college.

. . . I tried for many, many more than I got. I tried for a congressional internship—I didn't get it. I tried for a lot of international internships—I didn't get any of them. I tried for a Rotary scholarship—I didn't get it. I applied for fellowships, endowments, and on and on—I never got any of those. You name it, I applied for it and I didn't get it. But I did get a few things. For instance, I applied for a Glamour *College Woman contest and got picked as one of the Top Ten College Women of that year. I got to go to this big event in New York, was featured in the magazine, and met all of these people in the business. And to think, I had seriously thought applying for that contest was a waste of time. When* Glamour *called to tell me I won, I thought they were trying to sell me a subscription, so I said, "Oh, I already get the magazine," and I hung up. So even though I didn't get most of the things I applied for, I always recommend students apply for everything.*

Having gotten so much experience in college, Veronica graduated into an assistant entertainment editor position at *Essence* magazine. Then, for six months, she was a freelance magazine article writer.

I figured out there was a direct proportion between how many pitch letters you sent out and how many responses you got back. Ten pitch letters would get me two assignments . . . I ended up working at Premiere, *but I pitched them repeatedly, repeatedly, and repeatedly! Finally, after a year and twelve letters, I came home to a message on my machine that said, "I liked your ideas . . . Call me. I want to give you a story." That was the greatest feeling.*

" Whenever I met an editor or someone I might want to work with, I'd put them on my mailing list and I'd write them a note every couple of months to tell them what I was working on. It's weird because it makes me sound like Attila the Hun but I'm not. "
VERONICA CHAMBERS

" I've tried everything so it just looks like I've had more successes than failures. "
VERONICA CHAMBERS

" I was waiting for someone to say, 'Oh Veronica, you're so smart and you're so special, come work at my magazine.' But the thing is you don't need to wait for someone to pick you out of a crowd. You can go out there and do your thing and eventually you find your own star and it seems as if you've been picked out of a crowd. "
VERONICA CHAMBERS

By age twenty-three, Veronica Chambers was story editor for the well-known publication *New York Times Magazine* and was on top of her world.

> *I love what I do. I love the fact that my job is to find great ideas and great writers. And there's a publishing house that is paying me money to write a book. It's fun and you just want more. It's my dream job and it's a great life.*

Any secret tips for aspiring writers?   *research*

> *When I wanted to do an article for* Seventeen, *I went to the library and got six months' worth of issues and read them all to come up with ideas that they hadn't done before. Then I would write my pitch letter.*

As her tip for aspiring writers demonstrates, Veronica Chambers would qualify herself for jobs by really getting into the subject matter. Reading books and articles is a great starting place to master the subject at hand, but there are many additional ways to really get into your favorite subject.

Here are seventeen ways to "really get into" your subject and establish your expertise:

1. Google everything you can about the subject. Find out who the big players in the game are, where they are located, and what they are looking for in new employees.

2. Organize all the articles you find in a three-ring binder.

3. Start a http://myspace.com or www.facebook.com group to network with like-minded people and share stories and experiences. **?**

The only person who is educated is the one who has learned how to learn and change. CARL ROGERS AND JEROME FREIBERG, *authors of* Freedom to Learn *(Macmillan)*

Learning is a process of preparing to deal with new situations. ALVIN TOFFLER, *author of* Future Shock *(Bantam Books)*

4. Read the books written by the experts in the field.

5. Do an informational interview with someone who's already an expert.

6. Attend a conference about the subject matter.

7. Take a seminar or workshop that might be offered off campus.

8. Put your thoughts about the subject on paper, then turn them into handouts.

9. Get involved in online "forums" about the subject matter. ("Forums" are where people with similar interests chat and share information.)

10. Take a factory tour if you're interested in something that's manufactured.

11. Take a company tour.

12. Subscribe to a subject-related magazine.

13. Take things you learn and try applying them right away.

14. Associate with people in the field (join the professional club they're in).

15. Get a job of any sort that puts you around the experts.

16. Ask your professors questions about the subject.

17. Talk about the subject with your friends—it's good practice.

6 6 What real filmmakers do is they study films, they study their craft. No matter how much success they encounter, they are always in the process of studying. **9 9**
JOHN SINGLETON, *movie director who continues to watch at least one film a day, a practice he equates with taking vitamins*

HOT TIP: Check out the professional networking website www.linkedin.com. It is like a MySpace for professionals and offers tons of great contacts.

There is one extremely hot way to Really Get Into It that will also massively up your expertise: trade journals. If you get into trade journals while you're still in college, you'll be way ahead of the job-seeking pack. Most people don't discover them until two to three years out of college. One of the best things about trade journals is that they're free. All you have to do is correctly fill out the bingo cards in a trade journal that interests you and you're all set. I have personally subscribed to trade journals because they keep you up-to-date on industry trends, the important companies and products in the industry, emerging markets and research, how-to articles, hot fields, salary surveys, top 500 company listings, industry buzzwords, and much, much more. Every industry and field has at least one trade journal, and it's usually free to people who indicate that they work in the field. Once you've identified an industry

HOT TIP: An extensive list of professional and trade journals is available at www.amazon.com in the magazine subscription section.

> **"** They recall automobiles that are defective. I often wonder why they don't recall diplomas that are over seven years old. **"**
> FM 2030, *futurist and philosopher*

that interests you, aggressively subscribe to as many trade journals in that field as you can.

Really Getting Into your favorite subject is your key to building expertise and staying vital because:

- No one will ever teach you better than you can teach yourself.

- Many professors are "out of touch" with what you need to know for your profession.

- Employers practically require that you've studied the job you're applying for by at least looking up articles.

- Fifty percent of what you're being taught today will no longer be true or relevant in five years. (Let me explain. Entire fields and

disciplines are changing overnight. Think of it this way: Would you like to be operated on by a surgeon who hasn't learned anything new in the last five years?)

The bottom line is that there are two great reasons to really get into your favorite subjects on your own.

1. If you don't, you'll have one foot planted firmly on a banana peel.
2. If you do, employers will gladly hire you.

I already told you about the time that I looked up fifty articles about videoconferencing and was suddenly qualified to be a videoconferencing manager. Then there was the time I "qualified" myself to speak to college students about career development. I went online and retrieved every article from just about every magazine published in America over the last ten years that contained the words "college" and "success." The search cost me about $50 but at the end of the search . . . Whiz-Bang! The computer spit back well over 100 full-text articles. Instantly, without leaving my home, I knew a lot more about my subject! (Admittedly, I had to read the articles and think about them a bit first.)

Look it up!

- Look up the things you want to gain expertise on.
- Look up articles and books about the career that you aspire to obtain.
- Look up articles about any company you're applying to work for.
- Look up things that didn't get talked about enough in class.
- Look up burning questions that your professors can't give solid answers to.
- Look up subjects that you find the most interesting.

At the very least, researching your interests will leave you with the kind of reward best described by science-fiction author Ray Bradbury:

If you stuff yourself full of poems, essays, plays, stories, novels, films, comic strips, magazines, music, you automatically explode every morning like Old Faithful. I have never had a dry spell in my life, mainly because I feed myself well, to the point of bursting. I wake early and hear

❝ I know you feel that once you're beyond these walls and you're employed, you won't ever have to think about school again until you roll down the driveway in your Porsche for your class reunion. But the fact is, you have to keep learning all your life or you're not going to be able to compete. ❞
HARVEY B. MACKAY,
entrepreneur and author

❝ Don't hang with losers. Motivate yourself by associating with strivers. You are likely to perform at the level of those around you. ❞
WILLYE B. WHITE,
five-time track Olympian

❝ I don't want to get to the end of my life and find that I lived just the length of it. I want to have lived the width of it as well. ❞
DIANE ACKERMAN,
author and poet

my morning voices leaping around in my head like jumping beans. I get out of bed to trap them before they escape.

Next you'll learn a great way to take all the information you gather and instantly turn it into a valuable resource for your future. It's exactly what helped one college student who started a national nonprofit organization dramatically impact the American education system.

CHAPTER 17

SHOW-AND-TELL

Excellence is the gradual result of always striving to do better.
PAT RILEY

Wendy Kopp attended Princeton University and majored in public policy because she wanted a major that had a real-world focus. During her senior year, she wrote a senior thesis paper that proposed an innovative and bold idea:

Solve the shortage of teachers in underprivileged schools by recruiting outstanding college graduates to teach in them for a few years. That homework assignment turned out to be the starting point for Teach for America, a privately funded, nonprofit organization, launched by Wendy, that five years later had recruited and placed over 2,300 teachers in underprivileged schools in ten states.

It would be easy to assume that Wendy Kopp was a perfect student, but she explains:

I didn't go to tons of classes and the ones that I did go to, I would either sleep through or write down thoughts about what should be happening in my extracurriculars.

What extracurriculars? It was mostly just one: a campus club called the Foundation for Student Communications. The FSC was a club that published a magazine and put on conferences, and Wendy said she "randomly" got involved in it because:

Someone dragged me to the club's open house and they gave me a mailbox, which for some strange reason I felt obliged to keep going in to check.

> **"** I majored in public policy because it's a very real-world focus. It's not just learning a subject area, it's applying knowledge to solve real-world issues. **"**
> WENDY KOPP, *founder of Teach for America*

> **"** I hated exams. I can't even tell you how much I hated them. I would become terrified before every exam. **"**
> WENDY KOPP

In no time at all Wendy went from checking her mailbox to spending forty and eighty hours a week experiencing something she'll never forget.

Flow, that's what was going on. People were just operating at the edge and it was inspiring to be part of a team that was on a mission to take the organization to the next level. It was much more inspiring than sitting in on lectures about abstract things that, in my mind, really had no impact on the present day.

Did she worry she was overfocusing on extracurriculars?

I never questioned it because it's where my interests were. I was just doing what I enjoyed.

She remembers getting the idea for Teach for America at one of the FSC's conferences that brought student leaders and businesspeople from across the country together to learn from each other.

At that time everyone thought that only the government could solve the problem of low-quality education. But I sat at this conference and watched all these different students from different academic majors express enthusiasm for teaching. That's when it hit me: Why not help solve America's education problem by recruiting bright, ambitious college students to be teachers for a few years? And, since I needed a thesis topic, I proposed that.

About the time that Wendy got the Teach for America idea, graduation was fast approaching and she was not exempt from worry about finding a job.

I had been applying for jobs in the spring, but I was totally uninspired by all the things I was applying for, like investment banking, management consulting, and corporate finance, and the only reason I was applying for them is because those were the companies recruiting at Princeton. But along the way I continued to research my idea for Teach for America and I became completely obsessed with the concept as being workable, and finally decided, a couple weeks before turning in my thesis, that I was going to try to create it as a nonprofit organization.

She started by boiling her thesis paper down into a business proposal and then sent it out cold to the CEOs of thirty major companies.

" I really learned more in extracurricular activities than from anything else and I put very little effort into academics. "
WENDY KOPP

" No amount of money, no matter how much it is, will ever compensate you sufficiently for remaining in a job that is drudgery and robs you of your spirit, or one that prevents you from fulfilling a dream. "
JOHN KEHOE, *motivational speaker*

My hope was that a couple of those proposals would land right and get me a seed grant so that I could continue to get by because I had no money.

The day after graduation, Mobil Corp. gave her a seed grant of $26,000 and soon after Union Carbide said that she could use their offices in Manhattan. The rest is history. Wendy went on using her business proposal, the one that started off as a college paper, to raise millions of dollars in private funding.

Consider an interview scenario in which two college graduates are trying for the same job at a nonprofit organization that focuses on educational reform. Imagine that the two candidates have exactly the same qualifications, with only one difference: They answer the question "Why do you want to work here?" differently. One candidate replies, "I'm strongly committed to educational reform," and the other says, "I'm very interested in educational reform. If you'd care to see it, I brought along a paper I wrote about educational reform." Which person do you think will make the most impact? Most likely it will be the person who had the research paper, because in our society, you cannot underestimate the power of the printed word.

In Western culture, people and employers assign more weight, respect, and significance to things they see in print or on paper. What will you have to show after graduation, in print or on paper, that demonstrates your interests and skills to employers? Most students will have only their degree. You can get an edge by gathering, creating, and saving items that show and tell others about your interests and accomplishments and by using these to enhance your interviews.

Good show-and-tell items

- Articles you've gathered that are related to the job of your dreams.

- Newsletters, flyers, or brochures that you helped create for a campus club or organization you were involved in.

- A binder that contains handouts from important/applicable classes.

- If you want to be a TV personality, get video clips of yourself doing campus news.

> ❝ The only way to survive these days is to do some shit and see what happens. Every now and then you do shit that, for reasons that are completely unspecifiable, turns out to be big shit. ❞
> TOM PETERS, *management expert*

HOT TIP: Never throw anything away that shows positive or unique results. Give it the grandma's refrigerator test—if your grandma would want it on the fridge door, it should go in your brag book.

> ❝ My grades were by no means outstanding. ❞
> WENDY KOPP

44 I struggled so immensely with writing when I was in high school. I would go through these painful and agonizing experiences learning to write. But it's the best thing I have ever done because writing is 100 percent of what has enabled me to do what I've done at Teach for America. **77**
WENDY KOPP

44 I've become completely inspired to have a truly fundamental impact on the education system. **77**
WENDY KOPP

- If you want to be a photographer, create a portfolio of your best photographs.

- If you want to be a computer programmer, write a sample computer program and carry it to the interview on a disc.

- If you want to be a graphic artist, create sample brochures and business cards, and organize them into a portfolio.

- If you want to be a historian, write a paper about history and attach some great photos, maps, or interviews. (Better yet, turn your ideas into an interactive computer program.)

- If you want to be a journalist, write articles for your campus newspaper and save them all.

- If you want to be an author, put together a book proposal or write some sample chapters.

- If you want to be a teacher, create a great lesson plan.

- If you want to work at a particular company, gather news articles about that company.

The list above isn't all-inclusive, so think of other show-and-tell items that might be perfect for you. Just remember that the point is to gather or create items that are visible signs of your education, enthusiasm, creativity, and productivity.

Two show-and-tell items went a long way toward helping me stand out among 120 people for a public relations internship at Levi Strauss & Co.: eight articles that I researched on the company and promotional materials I made to promote a rock 'n' roll band I managed part time. I should point out right away that the employer didn't take much time to look at any of the things I had brought in, but I was later told that they had made a strong impression. Think about it: When I said I liked the company, I had articles to indicate this was true. When I said that I was interested in public relations and promotions, I had the rock band's promotional materials to make it obvious.

How to present a show-and-tell item

Since bringing samples of your work is much like the childhood game of show-and-tell, it is very important to remember that the game is not just show. You need to tell about what you've brought in as well. You can't expect the show-and-tell item to do the talking for you. Bring your strongest work to the interview and when the interviewer is asking about your abilities, extracurricular experiences, or interests, tell your story and briefly offer the show-and-tell item as a visual example. Make this brief so the employer doesn't think you're trying to avoid speaking for yourself. If they want to take time to look at your work, go along with it. If they don't seem to want to look at the item, that's OK too. Don't push it, and confidently continue the interview knowing that it's good that they saw what you were talking about.

Lastly

Don't graduate from college without any visible signs of your education, enthusiasm, creativity, and productivity. If Wendy Kopp hadn't written down her ideas for Teach for America, it's highly unlikely that anyone would have taken the concept seriously.

There's one place in particular where you'll find great show-and-tell items, a place most students never even think of. In fact, one college student found out about it almost by accident, but it resulted in some amazing networking.

HOT TIP: An excellent book on the use of show-and-tell items is *Portfolio Power: The New Way to Showcase All Your Job Skills and Experiences*, by Martin Kimeldorf (Peterson's).

66 What moves men of genius, or rather what inspires their work, is not new ideas, but their obsession with the idea that what has already been said is still not enough. 99
EUGENE DELACROIX,
French Romantic painter

CHAPTER 18

GOING PRO

Chance is always powerful. Let your hook be always cast; in the pool where you least expect it, there will be a fish.

OVID

Gilman Louie's success story is legendary in the software industry:

19-YEAR-OLD COLLEGE STUDENT STARTS A COMPUTER GAME COMPANY ON HIS PARENTS' KITCHEN TABLE.

To back their son's dream, Gilman's parents took out a $60,000 second mortgage on their home. Over a year passed and the company hadn't sold its first product. Friends and relatives started saying to Gilman, "When are you going to stop playing these stupid games and do something serious?" However, by the time he was twenty-six, nobody thought he should stop playing games because he was now the CEO of a $12 million company, which gave America computer games like Tetris, Falcon, and Vette! By the time he was thirty-three, the guy who every morning around 10 AM searched his pocket for enough change to get a grape soda and M&M's had expanded his company, Spectrum Holobyte Inc., into a publicly owned, international, $60 million corporation.

Gilman went to San Francisco State University and majored in business administration. When asked if he participated in any professional associations during college, without a second's delay, he raised his hand displaying two fingers.

I was in Delta Sigma Pi, a professional business coed fraternity, and DPMA, the Data Processing Management Association. The business fraternity was a great opportunity to network—as a matter of fact, I'm

HOT TIP: Join a professional association and list it on your resume. Employers will be impressed because it's likely that they're a member of the association also. Plus, 99 percent of the other students applying won't even know professional associations exist.

still in touch with the friends and business contacts I made through it. It also taught me how to deal professionally with people on a social and business level and that was very helpful. The other association, DPMA, focused me on issues that directly related to my company—and equally important, it helped me to network with people in the computer software industry. I can't say enough about the helpfulness of both.

When you become active in a professional association, the rubber hits the road. For instance, if you told me you wanted to become a book writer, I'd ask when you planned to join the American Society of Journalists and Authors, because I know of no better or quicker way to: learn about your profession; network in your chosen field; gather show-and-tell items; stay up-to-date on the latest trends related to your future job; and be able to put an impressive activity on your resume.

What is a professional association?

Imagine a club of historians, a club of film professionals, a club of accountants, or a club of perfume makers. Such clubs exist. There is a professional association for every profession you can imagine. Literally, there are thousands of professional associations nationally and locally that are organized to help those in the field stay up-to-date in their career. They put together reports and newsletters about the profession and industry, as well as hold conferences, meetings, trade shows, seminars, and workshops. They are mostly composed of people who are already working in the field but often invite students to join them. Usually there is a membership fee for joining and there is often a discounted student rate.

How to find the professional association related to your career:

- search the Internet

- call and ask a reference librarian in the business books section for help

- call and ask a professional who is working in the field

- ask a staff member at your career center

- look it up in the Encyclopedia of Associations

HOT TIP: Newsletters are an excellent source of job leads. Online newsletters can be found at Topica (http://lists .topica.com). Subscribe and be networked!

HOT TIP: The best book for looking up professional associations is *National Trade and Professional Associations of the United States* (NTPA, updated annually). Its subject index makes it incredibly easy to navigate. Ask for this book at your career center or library.

How to get the most on a student budget

Conferences are a big part of association benefits, but it's not always possible for a student to afford the cost, as was the case for me during college. But you can still get many of the same benefits. Here's how.

- Locate the appropriate contact person for the association. Explain that you are a student without enough money to attend the national conference. Ask them for alternate ways to participate or benefit from the association.

- Ask for conference guides, exhibitor lists (companies to work for), speaker lists (who's who), and topics covered (what's interesting in the industry).

- Ask if you could get a list of the companies that attended last year's conference; this will give you an idea of what companies are out there.

- Ask if it is possible to get an audio recording of a workshop that covers how to get into the field. Usually workshops and lectures are recorded and available for sale to those who couldn't attend. Maybe they'll give you a copy for free or at a discount because you're a student.

- Tell them you're trying to learn about the field and its trends and requirements and that you'd appreciate receiving any handouts or information they could mail you.

- Ask them what conferences are being held closest to your area over the next year.

- Ask them if they need volunteers for any of their events in your area. Maybe this will get you into an event that you can't afford to pay for.

Hidden treasure

The most important thing you should have learned from this chapter is this: PROFESSIONAL ASSOCIATIONS ARE OUT THERE AND THEY ARE LOADED WITH RESOURCES THAT WILL JUMP-START YOUR DREAM JOB. Maybe you can't afford the membership fees that they

HOT TIP: Professional associations often have websites. Two sites to search for your dream job association are: ASAE & The Center for Association Leadership (www.asaecenter.org; under "People & Groups" then "Directories") and Scholarly Societies Project (www.lib.uwaterloo.ca/society/overview.html).

require but still, without a doubt, somebody who's a part of this association can help you get valuable information or handouts for free.

I attended the National Speakers Association's annual conference, and it was an incredible experience. Imagine not knowing a lot about your dream job and being able to attend one conference where people from all over the country, who have your dream job, are gathering to share information. Imagine getting to sit in on conference workshops with titles like "How to Land a Job in This Field," "How to Excel in This Field," "Changing Trends in This Field." You can get any and every question you ever had about the field answered in one day. Hundreds of companies are represented by people you can meet. It's very likely that you'd meet your next success coach or locate an exciting internship.

Do yourself a big favor by joining, participating in, or becoming acquainted with the professional association that is related to your dream career. In one fell swoop you'll gain access to cutting-edge information on how to excel at your work, you'll network with companies and professionals from all over the world, and you'll have a great addition to your resume.

> ❝ I'm a great believer in luck, and I find the harder I work the more I have of it. ❞
> THOMAS JEFFERSON

Professional Association Chart

Let no fears stop you. Go for a very cool and unusual job. There are an almost infinite amount of amazing jobs out there and a professional association for each one of them. The following chart is just a SAMPLING of the associations that exist. Remember, there's also a magazine or trade journal for most of the following careers that you could be subscribing to.

Professional Association Chart

PROFESSION	PROFESSIONAL ASSOCIATION (OR OTHER MAJOR RESOURCE)	CONTACT
Album promoter	National Association of Recording Merchandisers	narm.com
Animal trainer	Animal Behavior Society	animalbehavior.org
Art director for movies	Art Directors Guild	artdirectors.org
Bicycle designer	USCF Mechanics Program	promechanics.com
Bicycle messenger	International Federation of Bike Messengers	messengers.org
Billboard maker	Outdoor Advertising Association of America	oaaa.org
Book buyer or promoter	American Booksellers Association	bookweb.org
Brewmaster	Association of Brewers	aob.org
Business consultant	Institute of Management Consultants	imcusa.org
Cameraperson on a talk show	American Society of Cinematographers	theasc.com
Candy maker	National Confectioners Association	candyusa.org
Carpenter	United Brotherhood of Carpenters and Joiners of America	carpenters.org
Cartoon voice specialist	American Federation of Television and Radio Artists	aftra.org
Celebrity interviewer	American Society of Journalists and Authors	asja.org
Celebrity publicist	Public Relations Society of America	prsa.org
Chef	American Culinary Federation	acfchefs.org
Children's book illustrator	Society of Children's Book Writers & Illustrators	scbwi.org
Clothing designer	Industrial Designers Society of America	idsa.org
Comic illustrator	Society of Illustrators	societyillustrators.org
Corporate video director	International Association of Business Communicators	iabc.com
Costume designer for movies	Costume Designers Guild	costumedesignersguild.com
Demolition contractor	National Demolition Association	demolitionassociation.com
Dolphin trainer	American Association of Zoo Keepers	aazk.org
Ecology protector	The Nature Conservancy	nature.org
Event planner	Meeting Professionals International	mpiweb.org
Farmer	National Farmers Union	nfu.org
Fast-food restaurant owner	International Franchise Association	franchise.org
Film promoter	Motion Picture Association of America	mpaa.org
Fitness center director	American Fitness Professionals & Associates	afpafitness.com
Forester	Society of American Foresters	safnet.org

PROFESSION	PROFESSIONAL ASSOCIATION (OR OTHER MAJOR RESOURCE)	CONTACT
Ghosthunter	American Society of Psychical Research	aspr.com
Greeting card writer	Greeting Card Association	greetingcard.org
Handwriting analyst	Handwriting Analysts Group	handwriting.org
Historian	American Historical Association	historians.org
Holistic medicine expert	American Holistic Medicine Medical Association	holisticmedicine.org
Horse trainer	American Quarter Horse Association	aqha.com
Hypnotherapist	National Guild of Hypnotists	ngh.net
Interior decorator	American Society of Interior Designers	asid.org
Joke writer for comedy TV show	Academy of Television Arts & Sciences	emmys.org
Laser tag business owner	International Laser Tag Association	lasertag.org
Leadership trainer	American Society for Training and Development	astd.org
Magazine article writer	American Society of Journalists and Authors	asja.org
Magazine editor	Magazine Publishers of America	magazine.org
Magician	Society of American Magicians	magicsam.com
Massage therapist	Associated Bodywork & Massage Professionals	abmp.com
Mathematician	American Mathematical Society	ams.org
Movie critic	Online Film Critics Society	ofcs.org
Museum curator	Independent Curators International	ici-exhibitions.org
Music recording engineer	American Federation of Musicians	afm.org
Newsletter publisher	Direct Marketing Association	the-dma.org
Park designer	American Society of Landscape Architects	asla.org
Performer at colleges	National Association for Campus Activities or Association for the Promotion of Campus Activities	naca.org or apca.com
Performing artist	Association of Performing Arts Presenters	artspresenters.org
Photo editor of magazine	American Society of Picture Professionals	aspp.com
Private investigator	Private Eye International	pi-international.com
Product packing designer	American Institute of Graphic Arts	aiga.org
Professional speaker	National Speakers Association	nsaspeaker.org
Radio reporter/station manager	National Association of Broadcasters	nab.org
Scriptwriter for TV or corporate video	Writers Guild of America, West	wga.org
Stage manager	Theater Communications Group	tcg.org
Stuntman	Stuntmen's Association of Motion Pictures	stuntmen.com

PROFESSION	PROFESSIONAL ASSOCIATION (OR OTHER MAJOR RESOURCE)	CONTACT
Stuntwoman	Stuntwomen's Association of Motion Pictures	stuntwomen.com
Talent coordinator for talk shows	National Association of Broadcasters	nab.org
Teacher or educator	American Association for Employment in Education	aaee.org
Theater arts person	Art Search	tcg.org
Theme park ride designer	International Association of Amusement Parks & Attractions	iaapa.org
Toy manufacturer	Toy Industry Association	toy-tma.org
Travel or food writer	International Food, Wine & Travel Writers Association	ifwtwa.org
TV weathercaster	American Meteorological Society	ametsoc.org
Video game designer	Entertainment Software Association	theesa.com
Wilderness challenge	National Society for Experiential Education	nsee.org

You probably won't find the professional association you're looking for on the chart above because it's just a small sample of associations. That means many of you will have to look up the professional association that matches your dream job on your own. A good place to search is ASAE & The Center for Association Leadership (www.asaecenter.org; under "People & Groups" then "Directories").

Break Time

Still reading this book? Good for you! You're demonstrating persistence.

Nothing takes the place of persistence. Talent will not.
Nothing is more common than unsuccessful people with talent.
Genius will not. Unrewarded genius is almost a proverb. Education
will not. The world is full of educated derelicts. Persistence alone has
solved and always will solve the problems of the human race.

CALVIN COOLIDGE

Persisting to the next section of this book is very important. You've come a long way with the discovery of your interests and of activities that build your expertise and professionalism. If you're doing the things suggested in this book, you're going to get lucky. Maybe you'll get lucky with a really great job or acceptance into a great graduate program. But you can't do the things in this book and not get lucky because luck favors the one who works hard, prepares, and pursues his or her dream. So:

- you will be the person working the hardest if you've read this book and followed through on many of its suggestions

- your mind will be prepared if you've participated in campus clubs, spent time with a mentor, researched information about your interests, or taken leadership classes

- you will be the person going after your dream if you've tapped into your interests and decided the best ways to pursue them

In the Next Chapters You'll Learn:

- how to practically get a guarantee on a great job after college

- how to walk into any interview with the odds stacked in your favor

- how to plan shortcuts

- how to decide what the next step will be that affects the rest of your life

Now for the best job-getting suggestion you'll find in this entire book (according to recent college graduates). It's the same suggestion that got Jessica McNamara an extraordinary job right out of university.

CHAPTER 19

SCHOOL WITHOUT AN INTERNSHIP WILL GET YOU NOWHERE

Every moment of your life is infinitely creative and the universe is endlessly bountiful. Just put forth a clear enough request, and everything you heart desires must come to you.

MAHATMA GANDHI

66 Sometimes it's scary to be thrown into new environments and responsibilities, but as long as you have faith in yourself, you will learn and eventually succeed far beyond where others stop. **99**
JESSICA MCNAMARA, *businesswoman*

Jessica McNamara is a young businesswoman who has found herself in a great full-time job right out of university. While many of her friends are still working at coffee shops to pay the bills and hopelessly searching through job advertisements, Jessica is in the fast lane to success. How did she get there? One word: internships.

> *My internship was a very unique experience in that it found me. I ran into an alumna from my sorority who said she had been trying to contact me. Apparently, she knew of an opportunity that fit me perfectly. It was the beginning of my senior year and I was looking to get involved with something new, so the timing was immaculate. Basically the internship was to work one-on-one with an interior decorator that had started her own business in the area. It wasn't the design aspect that attracted me, but more the idea of running my own business. I figured the fact that it was a small firm would give me more hands-on experience and allow me to become more of a business consultant than design assistant.*

66 I had to communicate on a professional level in all my correspondence and sound like an expert on the topic. **99**
JESSICA MCNAMARA

Although the opportunity seemed to present itself to Jessica, it was really a result of her work that left an impression on someone. So when the opportunity came knocking, it was only natural for Jessica to be the one they thought of. The ball was then in Jessica's court and it was up to her to decide.

It was exciting for me because I was sought out by a friend who knew what my skills were. I had worked with her in a leadership position the previous year in college, and she knew that a lot of the skills we developed together were utilized in this job. It was also a scary transition because in college I had worked with mostly peers and advisors. The internship, however, was in the "real world" with people who had been doing their jobs for years and were significantly older than me. It was also a commitment that required good time management and a lot of responsibility, I couldn't just call in sick if I had to finish a paper or something else more exciting came up.

Overall, Jessica's internship was a pretty typical internship with a mixture of pros and cons.

The pros of my internship were similar to most—learning through great hands-on projects, establishing good connections in the industry, potential for a career post-graduation, etc. I was one of the lucky individuals who found an internship that was paid, most are not. Additionally, working in a small firm gave me more of an opportunity to explore my interests and observe all the dynamics of business working as a cohesive whole. Some of my friends that interned at larger corporate offices were disenchanted with their experiences being so narrow. As far as cons, the hours were long and the work was sometimes challenging. I was learning new skills and honing the ones I had.

Are you thinking about going for an internship but uncertain what to expect? Well, don't worry, that is how you should feel going into a new experience. If you know exactly what to do and how to do it, you wouldn't be learning anything new and you would be missing the point of being an intern. You can always go back to your same old summer job, and sure, you might be good at it now, but remember when you started? It took you a while to learn the ins and outs of the job. An internship is the same way and the quicker you learn, the faster you get to realize whether or not this is something you would like to spend the next ten, twenty, or thirty years of your life doing. The best approach to going into a new internship is open-minded.

I really had no expectations going into my internship. I went in knowing it was something new and different and hopefully would utilize the skills and talents I had been working on in school. Having an open

> 66 All experiences are helpful, no matter how big or small. 99
> JESSICA MCNAMARA

> 66 It is an experience to develop what you do and do not like about potential jobs. 99
> JESSICA MCNAMARA

perspective helped me get more out of the experience than I could have ever imagined. Since it was a small firm, I had the opportunity to observe the operations and make suggestion on how things could be improved. With time, my employer saw that my ideas were valuable and well thought out and began letting me implement some changes. I felt so accomplished and I developed a sense of ownership and continued to try harder and make a difference in the office. This is the reason I was offered a full-time position after graduation. My employer recognized that the attributes I brought to the company were worth hanging on to.

After all the long hours and important meetings with clients and business affiliates, what is the biggest thing Jessica learned?

I learned to keep an open perspective and to have faith in yourself. When this position was presented to me, my first instinct was to say no. I was not the slightest bit artistic and did not have an interest in interior decoration. Fortunately, I decided to investigate it more before making a snap judgment. I have since been able to run with the business logistics side and build a career out of it. Of course I am still involved in the design industry, which is actually kind of fun because I never expected it to fit so well. I am a firm believer that you must have faith in yourself and your talents to succeed. We all have a bad day now and then, but as long as you stay dedicated and focus on the positive effects that you create, you will go far.

Does Jessica have any advice for students who are thinking about getting an internship?

Try to get internships in anything that interests you because it is the best way to really see what a career in that field would be like. It is the hands-on experience and development that make a difference in the work world. Don't be intimidated by challenging or seemingly pointless tasks; they are all a piece of the puzzle that make up your experience and will ultimately make you better in the end. Although an internship may require a time commitment from your daily activity, it is intended to be short and not binding. If you get an internship and then realize a week later you can't stand it, that's OK and a lot better to learn now than after graduation when it's your full-time job.

DON'T EVEN THINK OF NOT DOING AN INTERNSHIP OR CO-OP DURING COLLEGE.

HOT TIP: Arrange your schedule to have blocks of time to accommodate a part-time job of ten to twenty hours per week. Students with the most available weekday time have an edge on getting the job. For example, schedule your classes Monday, Wednesday, Friday so you can work Tuesday and Thursday.

Students who have done an internship or co-op have the edge on jobs. Every other year, the California State University surveys its spring bachelor's and master's graduates regarding their careers. When asked "What is the most important factor in assisting you to find work?", the number one answer was "work experience, volunteering, internship" (56 percent gave this answer as compared to 13 percent who answered "academic major" and only 4 percent who named "above-average G.P.A."). Referring to students who have done a co-op or internship, E. Sam Sovilla, assistant vice president for cooperative education at the University of Cincinnati, said, "Their extensive work experiences make them especially attractive to employers."

> **❝** In today's economy having just a B.S. won't do it. Internships and co-ops will make students much more likely to be employed. **❞**
> FELICIA THIGPEN,
> *former recruiter for Intel Corp.*

Consider These Facts

- According to a study at Northwestern University, 64 percent of interns are eventually offered jobs with their host employers.

- A survey by Vault Reports found that 77 percent of all college seniors had completed at least one internship by graduation, and 55 percent had participated in two or more.

HOT TIP: Start your career working for a company with less than 250 people, because in a small company you can figure out every part of what the company does.

WILL WORK FOR EXPERIENCE

A SALARY MIGHT BE A LITTLE PRESUMPTUOUS

Lunatic Fringe. Copyright by Ward Makielsk · Used by permission.

COLLEGE GRAD

- About 40 percent of co-op graduates will accept a career job offer from one of their co-op employers, according to the College Placement Council.

- The U.S. Department of Labor estimates that 48 percent of all job connections are made through personal networking. Internships and co-ops are a great way to network.

Instead of rejecting your resume because it shows only academic experience, employers will take comfort in seeing that you have real-world work experience under your belt. While you're getting a great first job, friends who didn't do a co-op or internship will be searching aimlessly through dead-end leads.

Internships Are . . .

Internships are part-time jobs in the real world that are related to your academic and career interests. They typically last three to six months. The only time an internship might be full-time is over the summer when students are usually not in school. For a student, it's an opportunity to get work experience in the real world and academic credit. For an employer, it's an opportunity to get cheap entry-level help and a chance to help students grow professionally.

Most internships don't pay wages at all, some internships pay a little, but all internships pay off in the near future. My first internship with a small company paid nothing. My second internship with a large and prestigious company paid $6 an hour and then turned into a $25 an hour job after graduation.

Co-ops Are . . .

Co-ops are much like internships, except that they pay a salary and typically last over a year. Most co-op programs offer you academic credit for doing the work, and, on average, the typical student makes $7,500 annually. Also, co-ops are usually available to sophomores and freshmen at two-year schools, while internships typically are available to upperclassmen. (In case you were wondering, co-op stands for cooperative education, meaning that the employer and school cooperate.)

HOT TIP: If you can't find an internship you're interested in, remember that any internship will move you closer to your dream job as long as it is related to something you are interested in.

HOT TIP: Monitor your learning curve, not your earning curve.

How to get an internship

There are quite a few ways to go about getting an internship, but the most helpful factors are having campus club experience and a bit of persistence. Tabitha Soren went through a lot to get her internship at CNN.

I applied to a gazillion newspapers for internships and got turned down for all of them because I was only a freshman, at least that's what they said, so I asked one of my professors if he could help me and he gave me a contact at CNN. At the interview I had clips, articles I'd written for the campus paper, to demonstrate my journalism experience.

Seven possible ways to find internships:

1. Ask at your campus career center.

2. Contact the office designated to coordinate cooperative education.

3. Ask the academic department chairperson of your major.

4. Call your campus alumni and ask if there are internships at their companies.

5. Call your favorite company and ask if they have an internship program.

6. Log on and look for internships on the Net. Check out these two sites for starters:

   www.studentjobs.gov—It lists internship and co-op opportunities around the country.

   www.internjobs.com—This site lets you search for internships all over the country and the world. It will let you search by location or key word. There are hundreds of internships listed.

7. Consult these books (check your career center or library for them):

   The Back Door Guide to Short-Term Job Adventures (Ten Speed Press) by Michael Landes. This book contains over 40,000 listings of unique internships, seasonal work, volunteer opportunities, overseas jobs, and short-term adventure jobs. Find some online at www.backdoorjobs.com.

   Peterson's Internships. It lists over 40,000 internships all across the country.

> ❝ Do as many internships as possible. My friend Marney had six during college. Intern somewhere for a month! Intern anywhere! ❞
> DAVE EGGERS

HOT TIP: Get a written job description for your internship or co-op and save it because you can use that job description to describe the internship on your resume.

A few people who did internships:

Connie Chung
Bill Clinton
Nancy Collins
Patrick Ewing
Calvin Klein
Spike Lee
David Letterman
Tabitha Soren
George Stephanopoulos
Oprah Winfrey

The Internship Bible by Mark Oldman and Samer Hamadeh. Lists over 100,000 internships.

An alternative option

If for some reason you don't do an internship or co-op, you can work for a temporary employment agency during your summer break. Organizations always need temporary workers to do various kinds of entry-level work. You can get temp jobs by looking under "Employment Agencies" in the yellow pages and calling for a few appointments. Once you start working for an agency, they will start sending you out on jobs that last typically between one and five days, but occasionally even longer.

On top of temporary work providing you with fairly steady summer employment, it is not unusual for temps to get offered permanent work once they've proven themselves on the job. And like co-ops, you gain practical work experience, you get to work in a variety of environments, you enhance your skills, and you get paid. Much better experience for your resume than working as a waitress or waiter.

One last thing

Remember, you're doing an internship to gain valuable experience. You can expect to do a lot of clerical work mixed in with some higher level tasks. When you feel that you're not learning much from the internship, it's time to ask your supervisor to increase your responsibilities. If your responsibilities don't get upped, leave the internship for another one. The company that you're interning for will often want to keep you working a long time because you provide inexpensive help for them. Don't be slave labor and don't stay in a dead-end position even if they offer you more money. Gravitate to situations where you'll learn a lot. Learn everything you can and then leave when the learning's done. Keep your learning curve steep and in a few short years you'll be worth more (and earn far more) than if you had stayed in a comfortable, dead-end job.

Once you've found internships or co-ops that you'd like to apply for, you'll be at a point where you need to know exactly how to set things up so that you win the job you want. I think the easiest way to win a job is to stack the odds in your favor by following a surefire, nine-step, ultra interview plan.

HOT TIP: Your time commitment to an internship is typically ten to fifteen hours per week for one quarter/semester.

HOT TIP: Already graduated? It's not too late. Many companies offer post-BA internships in fields such as business, technical, government, and nonprofit agencies.

HOT TIP: Internships that allow you to work with people at higher executive levels are better. Higher level people have more ability to get you a permanent position, create a job, or find someone who would want to hire you.

CHAPTER 20

THE SUREFIRE, NINE-STEP, ULTRA INTERVIEW PLAN

It is not the mountain we conquer but ourselves.

SIR EDMUND HILLARY, first man to climb Mt. Everest

Harvey B. Mackay, best-selling author and president of Mackay Envelope Corp., tells the true story of a young man who came to interview for a job at his company.

I asked him right off the bat what he had done to prepare for the interview. He said he'd read something about us somewhere and that was about it. Had he called anyone at Mackay Envelope Corporation to find out more about us? No. Had he called anyone who did business with our company? Our suppliers? Our customers? No. Had he checked his university's alumni office to see if there were any graduates working at Mackay he could interview to learn about our corporate culture? Had he asked any students or teachers for their advice? To grill him in a mock interview? To share information? Did he contact the chamber of commerce, go to the library, locate some newspaper clippings on us, or check us out in D&B? If we'd been a publicly held company, which we aren't, could he have gotten his hands on our annual report and any brokerage house recommendations? Did he write us a letter before he came in to tell us about himself, what he's doing to prepare for the interview and why he'd be right for the job? Was that letter a custom-made piece, for us and us only, not an all-purpose flyer? Did it show us his communication skills, his knowledge of our company, his eagerness to join us, and what he had to offer? Was he planning to follow up after the interview, write us another letter indicating his continued high level of interest in the job? Had he planned a way to make sure the letter would be in our hands within twenty-four hours of the meeting, possibly even hand delivered?

> ❝ Are you worried about pressure? I look at it this way: Pressure is having to do something you are not totally prepared to do. ❞
>
> HARVEY B. MACKAY, *entrepreneur and author*

In this case, the answer to every question was the same: NO. This left me with only one other question: The question I never asked because I already knew the answer. How well prepared would this person be if he were to go out and call a prospective customer for us?

It will take you no more time to prepare really well for one interview than to wander in half prepared for five. And your prospects for success will be many times better.

Delivered as an MBA commencement address, Penn State University, May 11, 1991. Courtesy of Harvey B. Mackay and Vital Speeches of the Day

HOT TIP: Less than 10 percent of job offers are generated solely by resumes. Make sure you know how to interview well.

Most people are under the false impression that a resume and cover letter are the keys to winning a job. Actually, your resume and cover letter are only a small part of what impresses an employer. Here's how to cover all the bases for an interview. I call it the SUREFIRE, NINE-STEP, ULTRA INTERVIEW PLAN and I caution you to use it only when you really, really want to win the job!

This plan wins jobs. But executing the plan takes considerable effort. If you don't want to spend much time preparing, I recommend you skip the interview because you'll probably lose the job to someone who really wants it. If you aren't motivated to do extra work for this job, go find another opportunity that you want bad enough to prepare for. Look at it like a game; you need to warm up before the big match!

⁜ Once you're prepared, you never know what roads will open up. And if you're prepared, it does not matter. If there's a road, you can pursue it. If there's no road, you can carve it through bushes. ⁜
JESSE JACKSON,
minister and activist

The surefire, nine-step, ultra interview plan

1.   Look up articles about the field of interest.

2.   Go on an informational interview with someone in a similar position.

3. Investigate the company where you're applying.

4. Write a great resume and cover letter.

5. Bring a show-and-tell item.

6. Dress appropriately for that job environment.

7. Practice interviewing at your career center.

8. In the interview, rely heavily on good human relations principles.

9. Follow up with a thank-you letter sent the same day.

OK, so you really, really want the job and you're willing to put in some extra effort. Here's how to make your plan work:

1. Look up articles about the field of interest.

Start by getting on your computer or going to the library and looking up articles about the field of interest. This is the starting point because knowledge about the field is very important and articles that you've looked up will help you converse in the interview.

2. Go on an informational interview with someone in a similar position.

When it's time for the real interview, you want to know what the job is all about. If you're going to interview with the director of marketing, go on an informational interview with a different director of marketing. Ask this person what professional associations could help you, what magazines and journals you might benefit from reading, and what things you could highlight on your resume.

3. Investigate the company you're applying to.

If you go to an interview without having investigated the company, you might as well also show up late. Don't get yourself into an embarrassing situation like the student in Harvey B. Mackay's story. Call to find out more about the company. Check with your alumni office to see if you can do an informational interview with any graduates who are already working there. Go to the library and locate some newspaper clippings.

HOT TIP: Don't wear cologne or perfume. Recruiters often mention not liking it. Freshly showered is enough.

❝ I go on my first job interview, and the guy interviewing me is a complete maniac. He goes, 'What do you want to be? A disc jockey?' I go, 'Yah.' And he goes, 'What are you? An asshole? Stupid?' And I go, 'No, I'm not stupid. In fact, I'm a graduate of Boston University.' ❞
HOWARD STERN

HOT TIP: In your cover letters and follow-up letters, don't use overconfident statements like, "I look forward to helping you lead Pacific Industries into the twenty-first century."

HOT TIP: Attention-getting gimmicks aren't usually well received—gimmicks like pop-up and fold-out multicolored resumes, homemade videos, helium balloons, attempts at humor, and packages of goodies. Employers see them as too "slick." Better to stick to the Surefire Plan.

HOT TIP: Call and request a good sample cover letter and resume from someone who works in a similar position to the one that you're applying for.

HOT TIP: Save papers you do during college because if they're well written and applicable to the job you want, they make good show-and-tell items.

HOT TIP: If you don't like the person you're going to be working with—don't take the job!

Get your hands on the annual report. Find out everything you can about the company before the interview!

4. Write a great resume and cover letter.

There are many aspects to putting together a great resume and cover letter, and I suggest you get custom, professional advice from a counselor at your career center. But I can tell you that a mind-blowing resume includes: campus club experience, leadership experience, study abroad experience, work experience, membership in a professional association, and an internship or co-op. A great cover letter would give two specific examples of how your skills and abilities match the job's description needs.

5. Bring a show-and-tell item.

This is a biggie that most people miss. If you create something, you can show it to the interviewer and they'll be able to see that you are creative, productive, and serious about your interests. Maybe it's something you created for your campus club, or a relevant paper you did, or the articles you gathered in step one.

6. Dress appropriately for the job environment.

It is important for you to do research on the corporate culture and find out what dress is appropriate. If you are interviewing at MTV, you may not want to wear a suit and tie. However, if you are interviewing at Merrill Lynch, you better get those nice clothes out of the back of your closet. Golden Rule: When appropriate, dress professionally. Research has confirmed repeatedly that professionally dressed people are always perceived by prospective employers as more intelligent, likable, and credible. As a college student, you probably don't judge people by the way they dress, but you'd be foolish to think that employers won't judge you by your clothing. You will not get jobs if you are dressed unprofessionally or sloppily. You will have a lot in your favor if you are dressed right for the job. In other words, forget about your personal style. If you're scheduled for an interview, drop by ahead of time to see how employees dress for important business meetings and copy them. This way, you'll appear to be a good fit and the interviewer will relate to you.

7. Practice interviewing at your career center.

A practice interview with a staff member from your school's career center is like a warm-up before a big race. It's an opportunity to get feedback on your resume, your outfit, and your answers to those "tough" questions the employer might ask.

8. In the interview rely heavily on good human relations principles.

Don Casella, director of San Francisco State University's career center, once gave me a very practical insight about interviewing. He said, "You can't prepare for an interview the way you prepare for a test. You can't try to memorize all the right answers. You have to prepare for it like it's a relationship." I know of no better way to do what Don's suggesting than to rely on timeless gestures of friendliness.

- Smile.

- Take a genuine interest in the other person. Encourage them to talk about their interests and passions by asking questions and listening attentively.

- Look for things you like about the person and compliment them on these qualities.

- Remember, the greatest gift you can give a person is to treat them in a way that shows you feel that they are valuable.

If you'd like to read about the art of human relations, I cannot recommend any book more strongly than Dale Carnegie's *How to Win Friends and Influence People*. Maybe the title sounds like "Sneaky Methods for Manipulating People," but I assure you, its advice is not about quick-fix influence techniques or power strategies. It is about basic principles of good relationships and enduring happiness. A more appropriate title might have been "How to Win Genuine Friends and Influence People Respectfully." A Library of Congress survey of readers named it one of the top ten books that had influenced their lives the most.

Interview Do's:

1. Make a warm impression by smiling and appearing excited to be there.

2. Appear confident by looking others in the eye, standing straight, and giving a firm handshake.

3. Avoid using excessive um's and ah's.

4. Prepare questions ahead of time so you are ready when they ask.

HOT TIP: If an association is on your resume, make sure you've attended a function or know what was in the last newsletter.

Interview Don'ts:

1. Don't walk in with a "know it all," egotistic attitude.

2. Don't exaggerate your qualifications or experience.

3. Don't start off with questions about salary/ benefits.

4. Don't come unprepared and offer lame excuses for it.

5. Don't give the impression that you have no career direction.

6. Don't come back with shallow or vague answers.

7. Don't say you have no questions for the interviewer.

8. Don't talk more than you listen.

9. Don't dress in anything other than your professional best.

10. Don't show up without knowledge of the job or the company.

Source: *Campus Connections* magazine, published by MarketSource Corp.

9. Follow up with a thank-you letter sent the same day.

Following up with a thank-you letter immediately tells the employer that you are professional in your communication and are sincerely interested in getting the job. Also, call five to seven days after the interview and remind the employer that you're interested. If you get voice mail or a receptionist, leave a simple message: "I just called to tell you that I'm really interested in the job. If you would like to call me, here's my number."

So that's the plan. Follow the Surefire, Nine-Step, Ultra Interview Plan and most employers will react as if you stepped down from a cloud and handed them a golden resume.

The following script is based on the true-life thoughts of a professional job recruiter named Thereza Lewis, who hires college students for summer employment. Follow the above nine steps and what you see here could be the thoughts that go through your interviewer's head.

Thereza at the Temporary Service Agency gets your cover letter and resume in the mail. Then comes the time to pick someone for the job.

RECRUITER'S THOUGHTS: *I have hundreds of resumes! Too many to look through. I'm going to toss every one that has a bad layout, typo, grammatical error, and a cover letter that's obviously a form letter. [Throw-throw-throw.] Okay—that leaves me with ten and only five of these state the qualifications and objectives I'm looking for. College students are so easy to weed out!*

You are one of the five selected for interviewing. You walk into the recruiter's office ready to interview.

RECRUITER'S THOUGHTS: *Finally someone who actually looks like they're here for an interview instead of a pizza delivery. Professionally dressed and a very nice smile. Now, hopefully she didn't pour on the perfume—the last guy's cologne was way too much.*

The interview proceeds and Thereza reviews your resume.

RECRUITER'S THOUGHTS: *Hmmm . . . a well-balanced education. She's had some volunteer experience where it looks like she got some real work experience, president of a campus club so she's probably a leader and a team player, and she has computer skills.*

From talking with you, Thereza finds out this job is related to your strongest interests and dreams.

RECRUITER'S THOUGHTS: *Good. I want someone who really has enthusiasm for the work. Most people don't know what they want but this person seems to.*

As the interview proceeds, Thereza likes the way you smile, listen, and act respectfully. She also likes the way you ask about her award hanging on the wall—it's something she's proud of.

RECRUITER'S THOUGHTS: *I really like this person. I get a really good feeling about her.*

Next you show Thereza the articles about the company that you looked up and mention that you talked to someone in another department.

RECRUITER'S THOUGHTS: *Wow, this person is ambitious and really interested in working at our company.*

Then Thereza discovers that you're a member of the Temporary Recruiters Association.

RECRUITER'S THOUGHTS: *That's the same club I'm in! This person seems so perfect for the job: experienced, ambitious, enthusiastic, professional, confident, self-motivated, and very easy to get along with. This is the person I'm hiring—I'm not even going to interview anyone else.*

Now that you know how to win the job you really want, you're ready to learn a super-simple planning technique that will enable you to achieve your dreams years sooner than you ever thought possible.

HOT TIP: Before doing a job interview, read a how-to book on the career you're applying for.

" Just be yourself, that's the only way it can work. "
JOHNNY CARSON'S *words of advice to Conan O'Brien*

CHAPTER 21

CHOICES THAT PAY OFF

If only God would give me a sign . . .
like making a large deposit in my name
to a Swiss bank account.

WOODY ALLEN, actor

> **"** Apply yourself. Get all the education you can, but then, by God, do something. Don't just stand there, make it happen. **"**
> LEE IACOCCA, *former chairman of Chrysler Motors*

> **"** A person is rich in proportion to the number of things which he can afford to let alone. **"**
> HENRY DAVID THOREAU

Up to this point we have covered some key experiences that are critical to a truly successful college experience, but there is another element that will play a part in your success that we have not yet touched on: financial management. Take the story of art student Scott Leberecht. Scott utilized smart financial management to enable him to meet the experts and geniuses who were responsible for the eye-popping scenes in such movies as *Star Wars* and *Jurassic Park*.

Scott walked the halls of the University of Cincinnati with a burning desire to work at the most prestigious special effects company in the world, Industrial Light and Magic. All of his heroes were moviemakers, and most of them worked at ILM; after all, it was founded and run by the creator of *Star Wars*, George Lucas. Scott held on to his dream throughout college, even after applying and being rejected for an ILM internship in the spring semester of his sophomore year.

One fateful day, Scott was walking down the hall on his way home from class, when he was stopped dead in his tracks by a poster that said, "The Making of Jurassic Park: Your opportunity to meet and learn from the pros who made the highest grossing movie ever." It was a four-day conference held during the summer in Hawaii.

I couldn't believe my eyes. I desperately wanted to attend that conference," Scott recalls. "I knew I would meet people from ILM there. But it was 5,000 miles away and cost more than I had in the bank.

He dashed back to his residence-hall room and tried to think of ways he could somehow afford the trip. The first call he made was to a travel agent who informed him that he could get a supersaver fare of $631, but only if he purchased his ticket by the next day. Scott was in a jam. He didn't have $631 to spare—and he wouldn't be able to earn that kind of money until midway through the summer.

It came down to this: The only way he'd be able to attend the conference was by charging it to his credit card and working a summer job to pay off the debt before the start of the next school year.

Scott remembers his decision well:

I was Mr. Pay-It-Off-in-Full-at-the-End-of-the-Month because nobody was going to bail me out if I got in over my head. Charging this conference to my card meant I'd be going into debt and that I'd have to work a summer job and save my money—so I decided to think about my decision overnight. When I woke up the next morning, the first thought that raced through my mind was this statement that I'd read somewhere: "It comes down to the question, What are you willing to sacrifice to get what you desire?" I was willing to sacrifice almost all my free time during the summer for a shot at ILM.

Scott rolled out of bed and made two calls—one to his old boss to line up a summer job, and another to a travel agent to charge a ticket to Hawaii on his credit card. Ninety-seven days later Scott was in Hawaii, mingling, shaking hands, and learning from the moviemaking superstars he'd read about since he was a kid.

Being there made me realize that the people in Hollywood weren't as different as I thought. It gave me a sense that I could accomplish things similar to what they had accomplished.

On top of the boost in confidence, Scott met many people who worked at ILM, and they gave him helpful hints for getting an internship at their company. Then, seven months after returning from the conference, Scott got the big payoff—an internship in the ILM art department. Even bigger than that, ten months after graduating from college, Scott was hired to be a full-time art director at ILM and was soon working on Arnold Schwarzenegger's film *Eraser*.

HOT TIP: Stay away from 900 numbers that offer credit cards. They are usually scams.

HOT TIP: If you find a mistake on your credit card bill, immediately contact your card issuer and clearly describe the problem. Keep a record of your communication. You have rights.

To charge or not to charge?

While you are launching your career, it is also a good idea to start establishing financial stability. Credit cards can be part of this process. While you are in college, you will be bombarded with credit card offers. People behind tables will offer you free gifts, if only you'll fill out a credit card application. Letters will pour into your mailbox that say, "Because of your good credit history, you're preapproved with a $500 spending line." You may not have a "credit history," and you may not even have a job, but you will be able to get a credit card while you're in college. The point is, at some time in college you'll probably have to decide if you want to apply for a credit card.

I remember getting my first credit card when I was in college. When I removed it from the envelope, I held it in my hand and looked at it with awe, realizing that for the first time in my life I could buy things now and pay for them later. But I opted to "freeload."

"Freeloading" is when you pay the entire amount due every month and, thus, avoid paying interest charges. In essence, this approach means you're using your card mostly for the convenience it gives you, for expenses you've got the cash to cover. That's a low-cost way to use a credit card. There is also another option. Nowadays you can get a debit card, which looks like and can be used just like a credit card. Instead of loaning you money, however, they draw money directly out of your checking account. So, if you've got enough money in your account, you can buy it with your debit card.

There are three good reasons to use a debit card or a credit card while you're in college:

1. At times they are more convenient than a personal check, and they're often safer than cash.

2. Sometimes they are the only way to purchase an item (e.g., by phone or through the Internet). For instance, try reserving a rental car without a credit card—sometimes possible, but extremely difficult.

3. Some cards offer benefits on purchases made with your card, such as extended warranties, price protection guarantees, or airline travel miles.

Credit cards offer two benefits that debit cards do not:

1. They are an opportunity to establish a good credit rating that will benefit you after college (more on this later).

HOT TIP: There is a free list on the Web that names some of the lowest rate and lowest fee cards: www.cardweb.com/ cardlocator

Success is not the destination; it's a way to travel.
DENIS WAITLEY

The few who do are the envy of the many who only watch.
JIM ROHN, *motivational speaker and entrepreneur*

2. They can help you cover emergency expenses.

Use your credit card wisely, and you'll have a very beneficial financial tool. Use your card unwisely and you'll end up in a financial nightmare. Some college students make the mistake of running up credit card debt they can't afford. Nothing is easier than charging small things here and there, only to wake up some day and find yourself staring at a credit card bill, in your name, that says "Balance Due: $2,000." I chose the amount of $2,000 because that's the amount a freshman student in Texas named Michelle Raimey ran up in one semester. It took Michelle seven years to pay off the balance—and her parents weren't about to help, even though they had the money. It was a hard lesson for Michelle to learn, but one she says "taught me the lesson that credit cards are in no way easy money."

Credit cards can be easy if, and only if, you follow these Twelve Brilliant Ways to Avoid a Credit Card Migraine:

1. No matter what, PAY YOUR MONTHLY CREDIT CARD BILL ON TIME. Come hell or high water, pay it on time, even if all you can pay is the minimum amount due, because you'll protect your credit rating, and you'll avoid late fees that are often as costly as a small diamond.

2. Keep a written record of every charge you make with your card, as if you were Scrooge himself. Use the record to stay within your budget.

3. Limit yourself to one credit card. Two simply increase the odds of screwing up.

4. Avoid impulse purchases. Spontaneity and credit cards are a bad mix. Consider the purchase for a couple of days and do the right (fiscally smart) thing. Remember to calculate the REAL cost of your desired purchase: A $100 jacket doesn't cost $100 if you charge it to your card and take six months to pay it off. It costs $100 + six months of interest.

5. Reward yourself in no-cost ways. Just because you aced all your finals doesn't mean you deserve something you can't afford. Instead of spending money you don't have, blast a stereo and stay up all night with a friend.

6. Avoid shopping as entertainment.

HOT TIP: Notify your credit card companies when you move so your bills will still arrive on time and you can pay them on time.

HOT TIP: Never give your credit card number to a caller who says he needs it to award you a free trip or prize. It's probably a scam.

HOT TIP: Landlords often look at your credit report to choose among rental applicants— so always pay your bills on time.

Don't wish it was easier, wish you were better. Don't wish for less problems, wish for more skills. Don't wish for less challenges, wish for more wisdom.
JIM ROHN

HOT TIP: Employers often look at your credit report as a way to help them decide whether to hire you—so always pay your bills on time.

7. Don't charge beyond your budget for holidays, which is when most people blow it.

8. Pay your credit card bill first, before you spend your money on everything else. Having a perfect payment history with your credit card is important.

9. Pay close attention to notices from your credit card company. Sometimes they are announcing a higher interest rate or new fees. If you don't like the new terms, get a new card and transfer your balance.

10. Don't use your credit card for cash advances. Cash advances are far more expensive than normal charges. They have higher interest rates, additional fees, and typically no grace period.

11. Treat your credit card like a $1,000 bill. Protect it from theft.

12. Refuse to load up on debt. Because of the way interest charges are calculated, if you're not careful, you may find yourself in a snowball situation.

Danger! Danger! Danger!

If you don't use your credit cards wisely, you'll find yourself in financial ruin. Nothing is easier, or happens faster, than running up a credit card to an astronomical sum and not being able to make your minimum monthly payment (when you run up $5,000 of debt, your monthly minimums can be around $200). If you can't make the monthly minimum, then the ceiling comes crashing down on you. Suddenly, you'll be overwhelmed with debt, you won't be able to take vacations because you'll have to work just to pay your debt, you'll have a bad credit rating, and no one will rent you an apartment, loan you money, or sell you a car. Suddenly, you'll have no CreditAbility.

CreditAbility

You have a credit rating and people (including yourself) can access it through several sources. Before you own a credit card, your credit rating is based on how responsibly you manage your checking account, monthly bills in your name, and any retail credit accounts you may have, including gasoline cards. Student loans and car loans also affect your credit rating. But, once you own a credit card, your credit rating becomes based largely on how responsibly you manage your credit card.

Building a great credit rating shows you are financially responsible. After you graduate, it should be easier for you to buy big-ticket items that often require a loan, such as a house, a car, or a boat. Some day, you may even want to use your good credit to borrow seed money to start your own business. Remember, while building a good credit rating is important, at the same time, you want to avoid anything that negatively affects that rating (such as missing or late payments). Good credit takes too long to establish not to use it wisely.

There are additional consequences for having a sloppy payment history. Gone are the credit line increases when you need them, "No Annual Fee!" offers, and the low-interest rate offers. Mess up, and you will be saddled with the worst credit card terms known to man.

Signs that you are getting into credit card trouble:

- You don't know how much you owe until your bills arrive.

- You're using credit card cash advances to pay bills.

- You're getting calls or letters from your creditors about overdue bills.

- You're often paying your bills late.

- Your credit cards are being revoked.

- You're only paying the minimum payment required.

- Your pulse quickens when you total up your debt.

HOT TIP: Never write your credit card number on your check. You are not obligated to give the merchant this information.

HOT TIP: There is no reason for a merchant to require you to provide your phone number and address as a condition of making a purchase with your credit card.

❝ Put all your eggs in one basket and WATCH THAT BASKET! ❞
MARK TWAIN

HOT TIP: Don't use your credit card to pay for 900 numbers unless you're filthy rich—no matter how low the "advertised rate" is, 900 calls are always super expensive.

A Gallup survey shows that handling an emergency situation is the #1 reason Americans carry credit cards.

HOT TIP: If your card is lost or stolen, report it immediately to your card issuer because then your liability for unauthorized uses will be $50 tops.

HOT TIP: Never ever loan your credit card or number to a friend, relative, or roommate. If you "give it out" it does not qualify as an "unauthorized use" and you'll be responsible for the full amount charged.

More words of advice: Each month, pay more than the minimum payment to avoid paying more in the end. Robert McKinley, president of RAM Research, offers this cautionary example: Let's say you owe $2,000 on a credit card that charges 18 percent interest, and you make the minimum 2 percent payment every month. It would take more than thirty years to pay off the debt, and you'd be paying about three to four times the original balance. Yowza!

If you find yourself in credit card trouble, the best solution is to immediately pick up the phone and get help. Call your credit card company and tell them the truth about your situation because they will often help you with a payment plan. Or call Consumer Credit Counseling Services (CCCS) at 1-800-873-2227. CCCS is a national nonprofit organization that can help you maintain a good credit standing with your creditors. They can work with creditors to restructure a payment plan. Best of all, CCCS's services are usually FREE!

Having said all that, you know how to stay out of credit card trouble. Next you're about to discover how to choose the best credit card. All credit cards are not created equal. Some super, super expensive cards may appear to be cheap ones.

The super-smart way to choose your credit card

First, you want to choose your credit card instead of letting a card choose you. Decide the terms you want and shop for those terms. This is generally what you're looking for in a credit card:

1. If you're certain that you'll pay off your balance every month, and I mean CERTAIN, then get a card with no annual fee, and a twenty-five to thirty-day grace period on purchases.

2. If you might carry a balance owed from month to month, then go for a card with a low interest rate and low or no annual fee. Interest rate offers range between 9 percent and 19 percent.

3. The final consideration can be the special benefits and rewards a card offers. But watch out, because the best reward programs may come with the cards that have the higher fees and interest rates. Those special "extras" ain't free.

CAUTION!

You'll receive a lot of offers that say, "Low Introductory Interest Rate!" These offers mean your interest rate will be really low at first, but after a while it will go up A LOT. Your job is to find out: (1) when the interest rate will go up, and (2) what the new interest rate will be. To answer these questions, call the credit card company and ask. An introductory period that lasts nine months to a year is good, and so is an interest rate that won't exceed about 14 percent. Remember, choose the credit card terms you want, don't let them choose you.

Payback Potential

Most items that students charge to their credit cards are often items they want, such as a stereo or TV, clothes, jewelry, $100 tennis shoes, food and drink, CDs, home furnishings, or 900 numbers. You can keep your debt down by charging only things you actually need to your card. To the degree that you want fewer material items, you are wealthy. It can be hard not to buy many things you want, but in the words of Bernard Baruch, "In the last analysis, our only freedom is the freedom to discipline ourselves." If you come to a point where you are going to acquire debt on your credit card and spend beyond your current means, think about charging only items that you need or that have payback potential.

> **"** The price of not following your dream is the same as paying for it. **"**
> PAULO COELHO, *author*

HOT TIP: Lost or stolen card? Call your card issuer. If you don't know the phone number, call directory assistance at 800-555-1212 and ask for your card issuer's 800 number.

HOT TIP: Free online credit seminar at http://creditinfocenter.com

Copyright by Scott Leberecht. Used by permission.

HOT TIP: Never write your PIN down and keep it in your wallet.

HOT TIP: Don't pay one credit card bill with a cash advance from another. If you're at this point, call your credit card issuer for help.

❝ When you've dug yourself into a hole, stop digging. ❞
OLD TEXAS SAYING

MUST READ: *Get a Financial Life*, by Beth Kobliner

MUST READ: *Personal Finance for Dummies*, by Eric Tyson

❝ You have all the reason in the world to achieve your grandest dreams. Imagination plus motivation equals realization. ❞
DENIS WAITLEY

❝ And will you succeed? Yes! You will indeed! (98 and ¾ percent guaranteed.) ❞
DR. SEUSS, *from* Oh, the Places You'll Go!

What are expenses with "payback potential"? They are expenses you incur now that will help you make money in the near future, such as:

- Quality portfolio materials
- Tools for your trade
- Career books
- Workshops, trade shows, and conferences
- Computer hardware and software
- Office supplies
- A nice business suit
- Business cards
- Subscriptions to trade journals and newsletters

Takes money to make money

Most of the time it does take money to make money. So if you find yourself in a place where money is truly a necessary tool for carving out your career and you don't have a friend, relative, or a financial institution that will loan you money, a credit card will do the trick. But you must follow these Three Rules for Powerful Plastic Use:

1. Only charge things that have "payback potential." Rather than spending on items you want, shift to spending only on items you need—items that have a direct correlation to furthering your career. Use your card to empower yourself to be a success. Then, later you'll have the income to afford the things you want.

2. Keep your interest rate as low as possible. Call your credit card company and ask them to lower your interest rate. If you have a good credit rating and mention a competing offer, they often will lower your interest rate—just because you asked.

3. Sacrifice, work, and discipline yourself until your dreams come true and your debt is paid off. Don't ever assume that paying off your debt will be easy—assume you will be able to do it with a focused and committed effort.

CHAPTER 22

FUTURE-PERFECT PLANNING

I dream my painting and then paint my dream.

VINCENT VAN GOGH

For some reason, many of us would prefer to skip paying the long dues that most people believe are required to get a dream job. Are you one of those people? Would you prefer the shortest route to your dream job? What I'm going to teach you is a planning process that dramatically accelerates your success curve. Believe it or not, it is a three-step technique that is taught in advanced business schools like the prestigious Wharton School of Business and in lofty management seminars where I learned it. It goes like this:

1. Picture yourself years down the road and massively successful.

2. From the future-perfect place you're imagining, ask yourself these questions (it does help to also share these questions with a person who might have more specific answers):

    a. What does my business card say on it?

    b. What kinds of books did I read to help myself achieve this success?

    c. What kinds of people do I work with? Are some of them famous?

    d. What magazine subscriptions do I receive to keep me up-to-date in my career?

    e. What clubs and professional organizations am I a member of?

    f. What skill proved to be the most important to my success?

> **"** The things I've done in my life have required a lot of years of work before they took off. **"**
> STEVE JOBS

> **"** Real motivation is that drive from within: You know where you are going because you have a compelling image inside, not a travel poster on the wall. **"**
> DENIS WAITLEY

> **"** Don't just do something, sit there! Sit there long enough each morning to decide what is really important during the day ahead. **"**
> RICHARD EYRE,
> *director*

❤❤ Most people spend more time planning a vacation or a party than they spend planning their lives. ❝❝
DENIS WAITLEY

g. What jobs got me to this successful place?

h. How do I dress?

3. Don't wait until the future—use your answers like a list and go shopping for the closest match you can get to each thing you imagined right now.

That is it. That is the fastest way to achieve your dream job. For myself, this planning process shaved a good two or three years off achieving my dream job of professional speaking. In August of 1992, I decided to become a speaker on college campuses. I was starting completely from scratch, with the exception that I could speak confidently in public. I had no speech written, no business leads, no money, and no time to waste—so I started with future-perfect planning.

I closed my eyes and imagined myself far into the future at a time when I had become a very successful speaker. From this future-perfect place I saw a lot of things. I imagined that I had an office and I imagined a lot of things in my office. The first things I saw were brochures that promoted my speeches. Since I was imagining myself as super-successful, I saw the brochures as super-great—full color, high design, and covered with testimonial quotes from students all across the country. I also imagined a bookshelf with many books about public speaking, motivation, success, and college; subscriptions to magazines specifically for speakers (although I had no idea if such magazines existed); and lastly that I was a member of a speakers club. I figured that the club was where I made friends with a lot of other speakers.

After that little mental exercise, I had my shopping list and I knew that if I wanted to reach that dream as soon as possible, I needed all that stuff as soon as possible. So I found:

College. Copyright by Dan Killeen. Used by permission.

- books (at the bookstore, online, from friends and mentors, etc.)

- magazines (at the library and my own subscriptions)

- clubs/associations (advertised in the magazines)

- speaking skills (I joined my local Toastmasters so I could practice every week)

- brochures (I got them designed by a young graphic designer in exchange for a computer modem and put the printing costs on my credit card)

- mentors (requested through the association and won with a little persistence)

Doing all these things took me about two months. Think about what I had going for me at the end of that time: I had enough tools of the trade to make speaker bureaus and college career centers take me very seriously. As a result, I got a paid gig three months later, for a fee that is normally paid to speakers who have been in the business for at least three years.

Doing this future-perfect planning exercise is like hitting the fast-forward button on your success. Instead of waiting for all these things to happen to you, you make them happen as soon as possible. And the sooner you get the items on the list, the sooner things'll get cookin'.

HOT TIP: Peruse the fantastic *Job Hunter's Sourcebook: Where to Find Employment Leads and Other Job Search Resources* by Kristy Swartout, editor. This book is incredibly thorough when it comes to listing resources you can use for your dream job—it lists professional associations, plus it tells you sources of help wanted ads, placement and job referral services, employer directories and networking lists, handbooks and manuals, employment agencies, and search firms.

CHAPTER 23

NOW GET OUT THERE!

The hall is rented. The orchestra is engaged.
Now it's time to dance.

CAPTAIN PICARD of *Star Trek: The Next Generation*

Are you graduating soon? Do the activities suggested so far in this book and at graduation you'll be in a position to get a great job. What? You're not sure if you want to work after graduation? Thinking of delaying your graduation date so you can take a few more classes or do a few more internships? Great idea! Take as long as you like to finish school. The working world will still be there when you finish. There's really no rush, unless you're in a hurry to make money or to reach your career dreams. Look at that course catalog and take courses just for fun (last chance before you're at work most of the time).

HOT TIP: These three books are filled with great advice and comprehensive lists of Internet job-finding resources:

- *Adams Electronic Job Search Almanac 2000 (Adams Internet Job Search Almanac)*, by Thomas F. Blackett

- *CareerXroads 2003*, by Mark Mehler and Gerry Crispin

- *Electronic Resumes and Online Networking*, by Rebecca Smith

Ready to go out and get that great job?

You'll do well if you've followed the advice in this book because you will have the skills that employers are looking for. You are also about to job search in a world that now offers a lot more options than the traditional nine-to-five workday. For instance, you can choose from the following:

- full-time work with a big company

- full-time work with a small, growing company

- part-time work for experience and money

- volunteer work for experience

- contract work on a project basis for variety

- starting your own business

In addition to having more career options available than ever before, you are also in the midst of a job search revolution, and it's crucial that you are aware and at the forefront of it. Computers are having a major impact on the job search process. More and more each day, companies are hiring people they have found through computer databases filled with electronic resumes. Going, going, almost gone are the days when companies place help wanted ads in the newspaper. It's more effective for them to call a resume database company and say, for instance, "Please run a computer search for a person who majored in psychology. This individual should have internship experience, be willing to relocate to Chicago, and be OK with the salary range we're offering." The resumes in the database that match the qualifications for the job will then come up on screen. So if you didn't get your resume into the database, you don't have a chance.

Next, you can increase the range of your job search by searching the Internet's help wanted ads. A great place to begin your Internet job search is at Job Bank USA (www.jobbankusa.com/search.html).

Next, you can increase the range of your job search by using computerized job bulletin boards. Many help wanted ads are now being placed on computerized job bulletin boards, which you can respond to if you know where to find them. For example, Monstertrack (www.monstertrak.com) is one of many organizations you can contact that specializes in helping students access online help wanted ads.

One last thing on the electronic job search revolution: You must think of the Internet as an additional job search tool—a way to get lucky. There is a big question as to how effective the Internet is for finding employment. A lot of sources estimate that people searching for non-techy jobs have a 1 to 3 percent chance of finding their job online. On the other hand, people searching for technical jobs have a much better chance. Also, there is another reality to getting your job via the Net: Frankly, the liberal arts student with less than a 3.0 G.P.A. is out of luck as far as resume databases go. The traditional job search methods still count, so check out your career center or library to scoop a great book on job search strategies.

Before you start your job search there is one more bit of information that might serve you well. It's a career trend that indicates you're likely to have more jobs in your lifetime than your parents probably did. The Bureau of Labor Statistics estimates that seven to ten jobs in a lifetime is the new norm, and that along the way you're likely to work in three

HOT TIP: Just after graduation is a perfect time to do some Short-Term Job Adventures! (http://backdoorjobs.com)

HOT TIP: Many grads are now marketing themselves as free agents. Employers become "clients" and jobs are "projects" as these grads move from one opportunity to the next.

66 There are those of us who are always about to live. We are waiting until things change, until there is more time, until we are less tired, until we get a promotion, until we settle down—until, until, until. It always seems as if there is some major event that must occur in our lives before we begin living. 99
GEORGE SHEEHAN,
physician and author

completely different fields. "Most new entrants in the job market can look forward to a career that progresses with all the predictability of a ball ricocheting inside a pinball machine," says Howard Figler, author of *The Complete Job Search Handbook: All the Skills You Need to Get Any Job and Have a Good Time Doing It.* What does this prediction mean to you? Simply that you can be the captain of your ship, choosing and pursuing jobs you'd love, but when the winds change direction you'll have to make adjustments.

Sometimes you'll make adjustments because things don't necessarily happen when you expect them to happen. Consider the story of Darron Trobetsky, who got his dream job at Nike two years after college. The story of how it happened is amazing.

Darron's journey to Nike began his sophomore year, when he became involved in a fraternity on campus. Little did he know that his involvement in this fraternity would later connect him to Nike. His journey continued when he did an internship at a small ad agency. Here he picked up a videotape of the Nike commercial titled "Revolution," which he would watch over and over, thinking to himself, "I would love to work at Nike."

After college he went to work for his fraternity's national office. "Every one of the ten guys I worked with knew how badly I wanted to work for Nike, so when one of them met a former Nike employee he immediately gave me his phone number." Darron wasted no time calling the man, and the man pointed him in the direction of a department called "Ekin"—an elite department of thirty people who know Nike products "front to back," hence the name Ekin (Nike spelled backward).

Darron called the director of Ekin and things went his way immediately—the director answered the phone and happily talked for forty-five

The Brass and Fern. Copyright by Steve Riehm. Used by permission.

minutes. The call went so well, the director invited Darron to travel to Portland, Oregon, for a job interview. Darron confidently accepted and went to compete with fifteen other people for five job openings. In a single day he did three different interviews that went great.

They called a week later and told me that I didn't get the job. I was super shocked and really disappointed. They told me I needed more experience in sports marketing. It was heartbreaking, but I thought to myself, "I'm going to be an Ekin someday. I just need more experience."

He found that experience at a track cycling facility near his hometown in Trexlertown, Pennsylvania.

I met somebody who was real important with the facility, and they needed help for the Olympic trials. I told him that I didn't care what they paid me, I was willing to volunteer. I got the job and was carrying cases of soda, writing press releases, and meeting with advertisers. Meanwhile, I kept in contact with the director at Nike, calling him to say, "Hey, here's what I'm doing—you should hire me." After a couple months he invited me back for another job interview.

Darron's second try at Nike was in New Jersey with ten people competing for two jobs. This time Darron shined like a supernova. "I hit it out of the park! It went really great."

But Nike gave the job to two other people and told Darron, "You're on our bench." Darron remembers all his friends asking him if he got the job. "I'd answer, 'Well no, but yes. I'm up next.'"

It felt like a real setback, but still, in my heart, I didn't want to give up. To make sure I stayed on the director's mind, I'd call or send a note every two weeks. I'd clip an article from a sports trend magazine and send it along with a short note. I learned through my fraternity involvement how much people appreciate a kind note.

Then in January, four months later, something went really wrong. The director who believed in Darron so much left the company. Darron had to start over. He worked to reintroduce himself to two new people with calls and letters. After two more months it paid off. Again he was invited to interview, this time in March, and this time at Nike's headquarters in Beaverton, Oregon.

"I went into this interview with a whole new level of confidence. I didn't even take pictures of the Nike headquarters because I knew I was

❝ Don't just go to school. Make an impact there. **❞**
DARRON TROBETSKY,
got his dream job at Nike

❝ I sent thank you notes before I left the Portland airport. **❞**
DARRON TROBETSKY

❝ If you can see your path laid out in front of you step by step, you know it's not your path. Your own path you make with every step you take. That's why it's your path. **❞**
JOSEPH CAMPBELL,
professor and writer

Nike receives over 100,000 resumes a year, though it never posts a job opening.

ff Take the first step in faith. You don't have to see the whole staircase, just take the first step. **JJ**
DR. MARTIN LUTHER KING, JR

ff . . . if we wait for the moment when everything, absolutely everything is ready, we shall never begin. **JJ**
IVAN TURGENEV, *novelist and playwright*

going to be back." Darron's first two interviews went well, and during his third and most important interview of the day, Darron noticed a bulging folder with a green card hanging out. It was sitting on the executive's desk. During the course of the interview, the executive opened the folder to retrieve something. Imagine Darron's surprise when he saw it was full of his own cards and notes. The previous director had kept everything Darron had ever sent.

Darron had been trying to get his dream job for almost a year—longer if you count the years he spent dreaming about it—and suddenly every ounce of his persistence was paying off. The third interview went great and Darron was finally hired to be part of Ekin.

There is only one thing we control in life, and that's how we react. I really wanted a job at Nike and no matter how much it hurt to get turned down, I was determined to work harder and be ten times better. Even though I didn't see it, I probably wasn't ready the first two times. But now I've got a job I love more than any other job I've ever had.

Maybe the greatest thing about Darron's story is that he never stopped going for his dreams. There will be times in your life when you'll suffer setbacks, but those setbacks will only be setbacks if you allow them to be. Persistence is a great habit employed by successful people, as is networking with courteous cards and phone calls.

Thinking of getting your master's degree? Caution!

Students start thinking about getting their master's degree near graduation for three reasons but only two of them are good ones. The first reason many students want to get their master's is because graduation draws near and they suddenly realize that they're not ready for the real world. They have no idea what they want to do, no work experiences, no job leads, and so forth. Because they're unprepared, they've decided to get their master's degree. It sounds impressive, it delays the pressure of getting a job for another two years, and they figure they will finally get the job skills they know they need. These students are going over Niagara Falls—a master's degree no more prepares you for work than a bachelor's degree did. If you're panicked because you don't feel prepared, the best remedy is to get out there and work for a year. Right away you'll get a sense of what work you like and don't like to do.

The second reason students want to get their master's is because so many professors recommend it. It's important to understand where your professors are coming from. A crowning jewel for professors is for one of their students to go on to get a PhD, and to teach and do research. They sometimes hope students will take the higher education path because it means they inspired you so much and taught you so well that you wanted to follow in their footsteps. And yes, if you do want to follow in one of your professor's footsteps, higher education is the required path.

The third reason many students want to get their master's is because they've heard that people with a degree get paid a lot more and have a better chance at getting a job. Some fields require an advanced degree for entry—for instance, law, medicine, scientific research, and college or university teaching. But if you're not planning to go into those fields, a master's degree usually will not increase your starting salary or give you a better chance at winning jobs, because employers are hiring based on work experience most of all.

So, the two good reasons for getting your master's are (1) if the career of your choice requires an advanced degree for entry; (2) if it's a dream of yours (and make sure it is your dream, not your parents' or counselor's) to get a master's degree. Other than those two reasons, you'd do better to get started on your career.

Thinking of taking some time off after college to travel? Go for it!

There is no better time to travel than right after college. You're still largely free from big financial obligations like house payments, furniture bills, insurance payments, and so on. And again, the working world will want you just as much when you get back. (They may even want you more because you'll have interesting stories to tell.)

Think it sounds unrealistic to travel right after graduation? Well, Charnae Wright liked the idea and she decided to backpack around Europe for four months. She met up with two friends from college along the way, and the group befriended quite a few locals in France.

I wanted to expand my horizons, see beautiful cultured places, and learn how other people around the world live. In my opinion, traveling is the greatest education a person can get.

So maybe you are interested in traveling but nervous to go on your own. Well then, talk to your friends and see if they would go with you. Look at it as a huge graduation present!

> *Not everyone can be born beautiful or intelligent but everyone can become effective. Yet there are very few really effective people. Any employer will employ an effective person ahead of any other person.*
> EDWARD DE BONO, *author*

> *You may delay, but time will not.*
> BENJAMIN FRANKLIN

> *Make sure you do your research and planning, but also leave room for spontaneity and meeting cool new people.*
> CHARNAE WRIGHT

> *The best things in life are usually unplanned and unexpected.*
> CHARNAE WRIGHT

> Far better it is to dare mighty things, to win glorious triumphs though checkered by failure, then to rank with those poor spirits who neither enjoy nor suffer much because they live in the gray twilight that knows neither victory nor defeat.
> TEDDY ROOSEVELT

Be sure to choose travel companions wisely. Not everyone you like has the traveling personality to help the trip run smoothly and take initiative to get things done. You see your travel buddies in every state possible! It is an amazing bonding experience, in both the positive and the not so positive effects! Backpacking brings about so many different kinds of emotions and having a solid partner or group can make the trip much more complementary to your style.

If Charnae had to sum up her entire trip in one word, what would it be?

If I had to sum up my experience in one word it would be . . . random. All by chance we met amazing people, stayed in unbelievable places, and did some of the most surreal things I can think of. We thought good thoughts, kept positive attitudes, and luck seemed to be on our side. That doesn't mean we didn't miss any trains or lose things along the way, but for the most part we had great group dynamics and very open communication. Every day was a brand-new experience!

After four years at a top university, what could traveling teach you?

I learned what it really means to come from different walks in life. I learned that the true character of people comes from actions and reactions to things in life that are challenging. I learned to be careful of the energy I was putting out because it was always going to come right back to me. And most importantly, I learned to go with my intuition, seize the grand opportunities, and let myself enjoy the very moment I am in.

What recommendations would Charnae give to students who are thinking about traveling after graduation?

Go for it! Connecting with people from different backgrounds, cultures, and experiences is eye-opening and life changing. That one-of-a-kind, irreplaceable growing experience is worth every penny. Once your mind is made up to do it, things start happening to help you make the trip a reality.

Read on, because the next section has the best stories in the whole book—stories that illustrate the six habits that will take you as far as you want to go in life.

PART 3

HIGH OCTANE

Desire is the key to motivation, but it's the determination and commitment to an unrelenting pursuit of your goal—a commitment to excellence—that will enable you to attain the success you seek.

MARIO ANDRETTI

The Six Habits of Students Who Will Go Far

Success. 1. The achievement of something desired, planned, or attempted.
NEW COLLEGE EDITION OF THE AMERICAN HERITAGE DICTIONARY

This book is building momentum and if you've been doing the suggested activities, buckle up because you're about to hit warp speed. The first two sections have covered how to get the most out of your education to prepare yourself to get a good job. The next part will show you what it takes to actually reach your dreams. (I kid you not.)

Each of the following chapters details a fundamental habit of success. If you want to make a million bucks, paint a masterpiece, solve the homelessness problem, set a world record, become a fabulous teacher, or launch your own business—the six fundamentals of success are:

1. The ability to focus on what you care about

2. The ability to make bold decisions

3. The desire to commit yourself to taking the time to make your dreams come true

4. The courage to break through your failures

5. The good sense to pay yourself 10 percent, first and always

6. Being good to others

Take these enormously powerful principles and make them into habits. When they become something you do on a consistent basis, no one can stop you from achieving your success. Next, you will see how one student used the technique in the following chapter to work in South Africa with HIV/AIDS programs.

CHAPTER 24

FOCUS—AND FOCUS ON WHAT YOU CARE ABOUT

When you are inspired by some great purpose, some extraordinary project, all your thoughts break their bonds; your mind transcends limitations, your consciousness expands in every direction, and you find yourself in a new, great, and wonderful world. Dormant forces, faculties, and talents become alive, and you discover yourself to be a greater person by far than you ever dreamed yourself to be.

PATANJALI

Most people don't know how to begin realizing their dreams. When they try to picture the necessary steps, all they see is gray. But you don't have to know all the steps to begin—all you need to know is how to get started. Starting is the most important part, and you can do that by picking up a how-to book about your profession or by doing an informational interview with someone who is already in the field. After that, you really don't need a detailed plan. All you need is a focus on what you care about.

Shortly after graduating, Sophie Cheetham concentrated all her energy on helping fight the HIV/AIDS pandemic. Her courageous story is a great example of someone focusing on what they care about.

> *I graduated with a degree in international development and a minor in sociology. During my time at university I focused on the social, political, and economic development of Africa. While studying this vast continent I became increasingly interested in the HIV/AIDS pandemic and ended up writing my undergraduate thesis on the topic. Through the work required for my dissertation, I discovered a real passion for learning about HIV/AIDS and ultimately decided to pursue a career in HIV/AIDS activism, awareness, and research.*

❝ I found that talking to my family and friends about my plans really calmed my nerves and filled me with a sense of excitement. ❞
SOPHIE CHEETHAM, *worked as an HIV/AIDS activist in South Africa after graduation*

149

With Sophie's new excitement she was ready to go out and get involved. However, it wasn't as easy as one may imagine.

To my surprise, finding an internship, let alone a job, based in Africa proved harder than I expected. After many months of browsing websites and making multiple phone calls, I was offered a position in the Cape Winelands District Municipality in South Africa. The position allowed me to be involved in helping create and implement HIV/AIDS and food security projects in the rural areas and farmlands in the western cape of South Africa.

As you might assume, the idea of graduating from university and heading out on your own to do HIV/AIDS work in South Africa is quite frightening. What was this decision-making process like for Sophie?

I was scared. Having just graduated, the idea of leaving all the comforts of home to fly to South Africa and work with an issue as big as HIV/AIDS felt like a huge risk. What would happen if everything went wrong? I had no idea what to expect and questioned whether it was the smartest idea to volunteer my time when I was already in debt from student loans. Many of my friends were moving to big cities and starting "real jobs" with high salaries. Fortunately, even with all this junk on my mind I decided to go. I wasn't sure what the outcome would be, but I knew if I didn't give it a try I would always regret it. When I look back on my life I don't want to be bogged down with regrets. I knew I really believed in my purpose, so I went for it.

There is a lot of work required to organize such a significant undertaking. How was Sophie able to stay focused and not let the enormity of the big picture get the best of her?

At times I felt overwhelmed, scared, and worried whether I made the right decision. I kept thinking about all the bad things that could happen, which seems like a natural thing for people when the outcome of a major decision is unknown. In time, I finally realized I just had to accept the fact that it was OK that I was doing something completely different from my friends. I really cared about the work and that was the most important thing.

Sophie's experiences in South Africa reconfirmed her priorities and gave her a better understanding of the life that she desires.

“ The more I experienced, the clearer my career aspirations became. ”
SOPHIE CHEETHAM

“ If you really want to achieve something, you just need to keep at it until you get it. ”
SOPHIE CHEETHAM

“ Our lives begin to end the day we become silent about things that matter. ”
DR. MARTIN LUTHER KING, JR.

I am not interested in pursuing a career that pays a huge salary or is competitive and stressful on my family and lifestyle. I know development work doesn't pay well, and that is fine with me. I am not in this line of work for the money. I am in it because I am passionate about making a difference. During my time in South Africa I saw exciting changes like governments being challenged and social stereotypes being stripped away. My experience was incredibly empowering and filled me with hope and a drive to work in a career focused on HIV/AIDS awareness, campaigning, and fundraising. HIV/AIDS is a global issue and it affects both the developing and developed nations. It is an enormous challenge, and one that I feel I need to be involved in.

Sophie realizes that her work down this path has just begun, but the important thing is that she has taken action and is focusing on what she really cares about.

Dave Eggers focused all of his energy on publishing and produced *Might* magazine. Michael Bates focused all his energy on business and produced a software marketing corporation. Veronica Chambers directed all her energy toward writing and ended with a publishing career.

Entrepreneur, speaker, and best-selling author Anthony Robbins was called the "solutions man" in high school because he was so focused on helping people change virtually any part of their lives. He chose to develop this one ability by reading as much as he could on the subject and speaking to groups as often as possible. (Rumor has it that he skimmed more than five hundred books and would often speak twice a day to anyone who would listen.) This singular focus and relentless pursuit paid off BIG. At just thirty-two, Anthony had two number one national bestsellers, *Unlimited Power* (Fawcett Book Group, 1987) and *Awaken the Giant Within* (Simon and Schuster, 1992); and when he came to speak in San Francisco, thousands of people lined up hours early. (Public speakers don't usually get that kind of rock star treatment.)

One of my most influential mentors is Leland Russell, a man who can (practically) leap tall buildings in a single bound. Leland graced the pages of *Life* magazine as a rock band member, was the stage manager for Billy Joel and many other famous acts, the founder and CEO of a national real estate company, and now creates highly acclaimed multimedia leadership programs. Leland once greatly contributed to my success by telling me that I scatter my energy on too many things at once. "Results are produced by focus," he said. "If you focus light on a single point, you

> 66 If you want to win anything—a race, your self, your life—you have to go a little berserk. 99
> GEORGE SHEEHAN, *physician and author*

> 66 What this power is I cannot say; all I know is that it exists and it becomes available only when a man is in that state of mind in which he know exactly what he wants and is fully determined not to quit until he finds it. 99
> ALEXANDER GRAHAM BELL

> 66 It's not what we do once in a while that shapes our lives. It's what we do *consistently.* 99
> ANTHONY ROBBINS, *best-selling author of* Awaken the Giant Within *(Simon & Schuster)*

get a laser beam. When you concentrate all your energy on what you care about the most, you'll get outstanding results."

I took his advice and chose to focus all my energy on becoming a great public speaker because every time I've seen one I've thought to myself, "That's what I'd love to do." When I made speaking my focus and relegated my other interests to hobbies, I suddenly started to get outstanding results. It seemed as if everything that began to happen in my life revealed a piece of new information about my career: Something on TV would spark an idea; helpful articles started showing up in the newspaper; ideas started coming to me in the middle of the night; books were suddenly available on my subject; and inexplicably, I started bumping into people who could help me advance my career. I began to feel that I was being guided toward my dreams.

What was happening to me was the "Volkswagen Bug" phenomenon: If you begin to look for a Volkswagen Bug to buy, you'll suddenly start seeing them everywhere! Remember, your mind is like a bloodhound. If you give it a single scent, it will dig up every clue in its path until it reaches its target. But if you don't give it a strong lead to follow, it will pick up a lot of false trails.

A speaker named Kevin Hughes recently reminded me of something very important. He pointed out just how incredibly unique each one of us is. Using scientific probability estimates, he proved that the probability of a person just like you being born is less than the chances of a chunk of gold spontaneously forming in a glass of water! In other words, you are a possibility that has never occurred before and will never occur again.

No one else has had or will ever have your unique combination of talents, experiences, and dreams. So don't waste that uniqueness. Maybe you've got the combination it takes to find a cure for AIDS or the composition for the next Mona Lisa. Or maybe you've got what it takes to do equally great things of lower profile or less apparent significance. Maybe you can teach students in a way that will change their lives or speak to groups of people and motivate them to do things they never thought they could. Whatever you choose to do, you'll achieve it once you focus on what you care about.

Remember, the person who ends up doing the best is rarely the person who was the most gifted to begin with. The one on top is usually the one who prepared, practiced, and was willing to make sacrifices to

> **" It's the constant and determined effort that breaks down all resistance and sweeps away all obstacles. "**
> CLAUDE M. BRISTOL, *author*

> **" I've always been able to write and draw, BUT there's a million people who have the same skills. Skills are such a small percentage of what it takes. "**
> DAVE EGGERS

> **" The happiest people spend much time in a state of flow— the state in which people are so involved in an activity that nothing else seems to matter; the experience itself is so enjoyable that people will do it even at great cost, for the sheer sake of doing it. "**
> MIHALY CSIKSZENTMIHALYI, *psychologist and author*

achieve success—in other words, the one who was focused. No matter who you are or what you have or haven't done, you have this guarantee: Once you focus on what you care about, you will become talented. Talent isn't necessarily a gift; it is a product of being focused.

All of the people I interviewed for this book admit to the difficulty of learning their primary talent. Yet all of them achieved their goals because they were focused on what they cared about.

Beat the system's imperfections

- The system said Elvis was an F student in music. Beat the system by believing in yourself more than you believe in the grades your professors give you.

- The system says G.P.A. is an important indicator of your future success. Know that G.P.A. rarely affects a student's life outside of academia.

- The system says you'll get kicked out if you don't pass. Comply with the system by at least passing your classes because, like it or not, a college degree *does* make a difference.

- The system says you are in school for pure academics. Remember to get some real-life work experience along with your schooling.

- The system says your selection of a major is all-important. Select the major that you're passionate about and pursue whatever career sounds most enjoyable.

- The system says go to class and learn. Take it a step further and learn from everywhere—classes, clubs, leadership programs, internships, mentors, friends, books, TV, and overseas programs.

- The system says professors can teach you best. Remember that no one can teach you better than yourself or another successful person. Learn from the best, someone who's already achieved things you want to achieve.

- The system says that only some people are creative. Be creative in everything you do.

> *Nothing is more common than unfulfilled potential.*
> HOWARD HENDRICKS,
> *professor and minister*

> *Commitment doesn't guarantee success, but lack of commitment guarantees you'll fall far short of your potential.*
> DENIS WAITLEY

- The system says your credentials determine what you can be. Do anything you want to do and don't let "credentials" stand in your way.

- The system says there are no shortcuts. Meet successful people, read success books, and find your own kind of shortcuts.

- The system says getting somewhere is important. Aim for somewhere, but remember to enjoy every step of the way.

- The system says you're here to prepare for the next test. Prepare for a successful and satisfying life. Make your *own* agenda.

CHAPTER 25

MAKE BOLD DECISIONS

I wake up every morning determined both to change the world
and have one hell of a good time. Sometimes this makes planning
the day a little difficult.

E. B. WHITE, author

Everything about the schooling process encourages you to act rationally and think slowly and carefully about all your "big" decisions. Granted, many decisions in life—like choosing a school or buying a home—require this kind of slow decision-making process. But there are moments in life that require big decisions immediately and without rational analysis.

For instance, if you're in a desperate situation, you have to be able to do something fast before the situation becomes a crisis. If you're feeling inspired to do something courageous, you've only got a short time before the inspiration will give way to fear. If the window of opportunity presents itself, that window will not stay open for very long unless you climb through. In each of the following stories, I guarantee you that if the person had thought long and hard about doing what they felt inspired to do, they would have talked themselves out of a good thing. You can't be perfectly rational about everything.

For twenty-four-year-old Wendy Kopp, hers was a bold decision to create a national teaching organization. She remembers telling her Princeton thesis advisor that she was going to get the $2.5 million needed to launch the project from Texas billionaire Ross Perot. "After all, I'm from Dallas, he's from Dallas. I'll just write him a letter." Not a particularly rational maneuver, but she boldly did just that. He didn't reply the first time she wrote, but one day "the phone rang in my office, and the secretary said the call was from Ross Perot. I thought at first she was kidding.

> *Great minds must be ready not only to take opportunities but to make them.*
> CHARLES CALEB COLTON,
> *writer*

But when I heard that Texas drawl on the line, I knew it was true." Ross Perot gave her $500,000.

Seventeen-year-old Bill Gates made a bold and irrational decision to pick up the telephone, call the man who was making the first personal computer, and announce that he had written a computer program called BASIC—which he hadn't actually written yet. Bill programmed for eight solid weeks to back up the claim he'd made over the phone. The results of this bold move? You know the rest. He is estimated to become the world's first trillionaire.

For Alexis Mansinne, following her heart meant making a bold decision and turning down a secure job with great pay. She was a few months away from graduation and had no job lined up, but that was fine by her. How Alexis's bold decision played itself out is quite a story.

> *I worked my senior year as a peer advisor at my university for the department of communication. Halfway through the term my boss decided to leave for personal reasons. Over the course of my employment I had become increasingly interested in academic advising and had been looking into master's programs in education. When I found out she was leaving, I decided to take a chance and apply for her position. I went through the whole application process just like the other outside candidates, and after many long interviews, I was offered the position!*

We aren't just talking about some basic job filing papers all day. Alexis would have been counted on by hundreds or even thousands of students.

> *I would have been the main liaison between the students and professors in the communication department and the university administration. My responsibilities would have included adding and dropping classes, handling wait lists at the beginning of each quarter, declaring the communication major, graduation issues, and academic advising. When I announced I got the job, everyone was really impressed! Most academic advisors are a few years out of school and have much more experience and most have additional degrees. At the time it was a really big deal to have a job right after graduation. That's always the hot topic in your last year of college—who has a job, who's looking, and who's going back to school. I was seen as really lucky to have that opportunity, and I was.*

44 A great deal of talent is lost in the world for want of a little courage. . . . The fact is that to do anything in the world worth doing, we must not stand back shivering and thinking of the cold and danger but jump in and scramble through as well as we can. **77**
SYDNEY SMITH,
clergyman and writer

MUST READ: *Critical Path* by R. Buckminster Fuller (St. Martin's) because it will expand your conception of what impact a single individual can have on humanity

44 Do not be too timid and squeamish about your actions. All life is an experiment. **77**
RALPH WALDO EMERSON

44 Be bold and mighty forces will come to your aid. **77**
BASIL KING, *writer*

Now here is where her story gets good . . . secure job with benefits and great pay in a beautiful location, and what does she do?

In spite of all the positive aspects of the job and good reasons to accept the position, I decided to decline the offer. This was a really difficult decision for me to make, but I just knew it wasn't right for me. After I really thought about it, I didn't really want the security of having a job right after graduation. I believe there's something very special about the uncertainties in that time of your life.

I also wanted to travel. I had been planning a backpacking trip through Europe and my employer wanted me to start work a month before I had planned on returning. That was just not something I was willing to sacrifice. They were asking me to give up a month of hostels and trains, spending time in Italy and meeting new friends, late nights out on the town and the chance to make memories that would last a lifetime. I knew that when I looked back on my life many years from now I would have regretted sitting at a desk forty hours a week when I could have been sipping wine in a local restaurant at a piazza in Sienna.

Alexis graduated from university in 2005 and pursued her dream of traveling. When she returned home there was no full-time position with benefits and great pay waiting for her. She chose to let that opportunity pass, but do you think she regrets that bold decision?

There is no question that I absolutely made the right decision. It was difficult to turn down something that looked so good, but once I did, I knew it was the right thing to do. I now have a great apartment in San Francisco, wonderful friends, and an excellent job. It wasn't easy and has taken a little while to build my life up to where it is now, but my experiences traveling were life-changing and I wouldn't trade them for anything!

One of my bold and irrational but successful decisions was to write this book. I was inspired by a newspaper article about a student who had written a book and instantly I decided to write a competing one. If I had thought more about the endeavor, I know I would have talked myself out of it. At the time I was in a different job, I didn't know exactly what I would write about, I had never written much, and I didn't have any contacts in the publishing business. But I made the decision to just do it and a year and a half later I had a publishing deal.

> **❝** Life is either a daring adventure or nothing. **❞**
> HELEN KELLER

> **❝** The opposite of courage in our society is not cowardice . . . it is conformity. **❞**
> ROLLO MAY,
> *existential psychologist*

> **❝** Ordinary people believe only in the possible. Extraordinary people visualize not what is possible or probable, but rather what is impossible. And by visualizing the impossible, they begin to see it as possible. **❞**
> CHERIE CARTER-SCOTT,
> *motivational speaker*

> **❝** I would go into a place and say, 'I'm a comedian,' and they'd say, 'Get out of here.' Then I'd put a fifty-dollar bill on the bar. I'd say, 'Just let me tell some jokes, and if people leave or I embarrass the customers, you keep the fifty.' The wager always worked. **❞**
> JAY LENO

Many of the biggest, most exciting things in your life will happen because you made a bold and irrational decision. Granted, it's the actions we take after making a decision that actually produce results, but it's the decisions to take action that set everything in motion in the first place.

The decisions we make every day shape our future . . . and so do the decisions we don't make. A lot of the decisions we shy away from are the ones that we don't know how we'd pull off. I only need to tell you this: Bill Gates didn't know how he'd get the software done on time or if it would actually work; Wendy Kopp didn't know how she'd raise millions of dollars; Alexis Mansinne didn't know how she'd find work when she returned home from traveling; and I didn't know how I'd pull off this book. Bold decisions are bold precisely because of the uncertainty involved.

Life is simply too short not to take risks. I worked with a college student one summer who had gotten his dream job—playing video games—because he made the decision to cold-call a company on the other side of the country and ask for his dream job. The bolder the decision, the higher the payoff. I think the boldest decision a person can make is to live life in an extraordinary way. Decide that no matter what you do with your life, you won't settle for "average," "pretty good," or "OK." Make a bold decision for yourself right now!

> **“** Don't play for safety—it's the most dangerous thing in the world. **”**
> HUGH WALPOLE, *writer*

CHAPTER 26

COMMIT TO THE LONG-TERM

There is no sudden leap to greatness. Your success lies in doing, day by day. Your upward reach comes from working well and carefully.

MAX STEINGART, networking mentor

If you really want to be successful, a long-term outlook is a necessary factor. When you plan your goals, don't just think about what you could accomplish in three months or a year—think about what you could accomplish in five to ten years. When you make a long-term commitment, the possibilities change dramatically.

Veronica Chambers got the amazing opportunity to cowrite a book with movie director John Singleton because for two years she mailed him something every two weeks. Whether it was a sample of her writing or an update on her career, she never asked him for anything, just let him know who she was and what she was up to. After two years of this mail campaign, the phone rang one day and it was John Singleton calling to offer her a job. That's what a long-term effort can do for a person!

In *The Man Who Planted Trees* (Chelsea House, 1987), Jean Giorno describes a man who lived by himself in the middle of a barren, sandy land. Every day the man tended to his sheep and planted a handful of tree seeds. Day after day, month after month, and year after year he did this—for over thirty years.

Do you know what happens when you plant a few tree seeds every day for over thirty years? You get a small forest and that small forest begins to grow and multiply on its own. Next, a forest changes the climate patterns in the area. Rainfall increases and puts rivers where there were none. Animals move into the new home and life starts to flourish. And finally, a community of people move in because the land is again

> *People usually overestimate what they can accomplish in a year and dramatically underestimate what they can accomplish in a decade.*
> ANTHONY ROBBINS,
> *life coach and author*

> *Rain puts a hole in stone because of Its constancy, not its force. I just kept knocking on doors until the right one opened.*
> H. JOSEPH GERBER,
> *entrepreneur*

hospitable. One man planting a few tree seeds every day for thirty years can produce those results!

The amount of time you're willing to commit to reaching a dream is directly related to the probability of your making the dream a reality. Being talented or successful at something is nearly impossible if you're not willing to dedicate a sufficient amount of time to developing your skills. But if you're willing to dedicate yourself to the time it takes, you've practically got a guarantee that you will succeed.

Let's say you decide you want to become a guitar player. If you say you're going to give it a go for a year, you're probably not going to be the next Keith Richards. But if you say you're going to commit to it for ten years, I bet you'll at least end up on a CD. As a matter of fact, you'd probably be good after only five years, but the second five years would move you into the "excellent" category.

Many years of daily effort creates pure excellence. Somebody once said to a master pianist, "I'd give half of my life if I could play piano like you." And she replied, "Good, because that's about how long it takes." Arthur Rubenstein, the great pianist, once said, "If I miss one day of practice, I notice the difference. If I miss two days of practice, the critics notice the difference. If I miss three days of practice, the audience notices the difference."

Almost nobody wants to work on something every day. But some people do it anyway. Greg LeMond, three-time winner of the Tour de France cycling race, explained why he does it: "There are many times I wish I was playing eighteen holes of golf instead of training in miserable cold weather. But in the final analysis, I'd rather win the Tour de France than play eighteen holes of golf. That's why I do it."

There's a mental trick that can help you see daily work as progress instead of as a chore. It's a trick based on the premise that people at the bottom of an organization think in terms of three months to a year, while people at the top think in terms of ten to fifty years. Here's the trick: Make many of your decisions according to their outcome ten years from now. If you wanted to learn to play the guitar, you might say to yourself, "Sure, for the next two or three years I'll suck, but ten years from now I'm sure to be great—and that'll leave me with plenty of years to enjoy my talent." A similar thought motivated me to launch myself as a public speaker when I was twenty-six. I figured I'd be a great public speaker, at the latest, by thirty-six years old and I've met enough people over eighty to know that thirty-six is still young.

> " My original vision of a personal computer on every desk and every home will take more than fifteen more years to achieve so there will be more than thirty years since I first got excited about that goal. My work is not like sports where you actually win a game and it's over after a short period of time. "
> BILL GATES

> " Success isn't something you chase. It's something you have to put forth the effort for constantly. Then maybe it'll come when you least expect it. "
> MICHAEL JORDAN

> " You bust your butt hitting balls, practicing chipping and putting, working on your game. And lo and behold you hit that magical shot. "
> TIGER WOODS

There are very few cases of overnight success. Most success cases—including rock bands who seem to explode out of nowhere—involve longer term persistence and commitment to an interest. Consider Conan O'Brien's commitment. "In the '80s I was doing improv in a basement and I told myself, 'This will lead to good things!' If I'd been realistic, I'd have said, 'Give up the performing thing. You're almost thirty. It's not going to happen.'" Commit yourself to reaching your goals, put in daily effort, and time will fly and your talents will soar. And . . .

Take Time

Take time to work,
It is the price of success.

Take time to think,
It is the source of power.

Take time to play,
It is the secret of perpetual youth.

Take time to read,
It is the foundation of wisdom.

Take time to be friendly,
It is the road to happiness.

Take time to dream,
It is hitching your wagon to a star.

Take time to love and be loved,
It is the privilege of the gods.

Take time to look around,
The day is too short to be selfish.

Take time to laugh,
It is the music of the soul.

AUTHOR UNKNOWN

> ❝ When we watch a great musician or top athlete in action, we see a performance that may take only a few minutes. What we don't see is the hours of perspiration and preparation that enabled him or her to become great. The Michael Jordans and the Chris Everetts of the world have talent, yes, but they're also the first ones on and the last ones off the basketball or tennis court. ❞
> HARVEY B. MACKAY, *entrepreneur and author*

> ❝ The key to Schwarzenegger's success has always been hard work. He pumped iron harder than anyone else, and then he threw himself into a movie career with such energy and determination that he became, against all the odds and despite his Austrian accent, the no. 1 movie star in the world. ❞
> ROGER EBERT, *movie critic*

CHAPTER 27

BREAK THROUGH YOUR FAILURES

Success is the ability to go from one failure to another with no loss of enthusiasm.

WINSTON CHURCHILL

" A person's ability to grow and succeed is largely related to their ability to suffer embarrassment. "
DOUG ENGELBART, *father of personal computers*

" I have not failed. I have successfully discovered 1,200 ideas that don't work. "
THOMAS EDISON

" A professional writer is an amateur who didn't quit. "
RICHARD BACH, *author*

What I think of as "breakthroughs," R. Buckminster Fuller called "Great Moments." What we're both referring to are those embarrassing moments when what you try to do goes painfully wrong. Like the time Oprah Winfrey was dumped as an anchorwoman. Or the time David Letterman's first TV show got canceled due to poor ratings. Or the time Johnny Carson told Jay Leno he wasn't ready for an appearance on the *Tonight Show*.

There's really only one remedy for mistakes, failures, and rejections: You've got to get through them. After all, success has nothing to do with not making mistakes. Remember, when you were learning to walk, you probably fell a hundred times, but it never occurred to you that you "just weren't meant to walk." Making a mistake is just like falling down: It hurts and it feels like a good reason to stop. But the people who succeed are consistently the ones who get back up and keep going.

I've seen a lot of people who interpret their mistakes or failures as a sure sign that it's quitting time. But I've also seen people who see their mistakes and failures as stepping-stones to the next level.

Consider what happened to Dan O'Brien. Dan was the probable favorite for winning the 1992 Olympic decathlon event. Because a gold medal was so likely for Dan, several companies featured him in their commercials, which were calling him the world's greatest athlete. But despite the attention, when the Olympic trials rolled around Dan did so poorly (on worldwide television) that he didn't even make the Olympic team. Talk about failure! Many people worried that because of such enormous public embarrassment Dan would quit the sport. But instead of letting the failure stop him, he opted to work out harder than before, and two months later he broke the world record. That's breaking through your mistakes.

Dan O'Brien is an example of how failures and mistakes happen even after you've become a winner. But Step One is getting through the many mistakes that happen when you're just starting out. Katie Couric, the anchor of the CBS *Evening News*, had an enormously painful setback at the beginning of her TV career. Her first big break came soon after college when CNN offered her a chance to cover White House news. She remembers "putting on my little blazer, combing my hair, getting to the White House, and I'm ready to go on, I have my earpiece in, and during a commercial I hear one Atlanta anchor saying to another, 'Who is that girl? She looks 16 years old.' I was crushed." She also had a voice that wasn't ready for prime-time television. It was too piercing and her southern accent was too strong. Needless to say, her first television appearance was her last for a while. "I still have that tape at home. I was a disaster," she recalls. But she didn't give up. She overcame her weaknesses by working with a speech coach. Three years later, her lessons paid off and she became a prizewinning television reporter in Miami.

Suffering the embarrassment of mistakes is a little easier when you remember this: The embarrassment of a mistake or failure passes quickly; the advances you'll make last a lifetime. R. Buckminster Fuller pointed out that every advance the human race has ever made—everything we've learned—is the result of billions and billions of mistakes. So when you see a person who's able to do something really well, remember that you are looking at a person who's made it through hundreds and hundreds of mistakes.

Jon Stewart, host of *The Daily Show*, has a story to tell about his initial failure. "My first gig was pretty miserable. I wrote five minutes of material, went up there, lasted three minutes, and got heckled. And my comeback was like, 'Shut up. I'm not an ass____. You're an ass____.' I was pretty crushed because I sucked. But to some extent, it was seductive, because there was a laugh or two."

My own personal mistakes are many and have sometimes been painful. Once during college when I was trying to write a good cover letter, my mentor essentially told me (in kind words) that my first draft was horrible. That hurt! But it hurt even more when she said my second and third drafts weren't very good either.

Facts:

• On their way to the moon, rockets are off course 80 percent of the time.

• It took over 16,000 practice launches before rockets were ready to carry humans.

• Babe Ruth struck out 1,300 times. On average he struck out once every game.

• *Chicken Soup for the Soul* was rejected by thirty-six publishers.

❝ It is inevitable that some defeat will enter even the most victorious life. The human spirit is never finished when it is defeated—it is finished when it surrenders. ❞
BEN STEIN

❝ Failure taught me that failure isn't the end·unless you give up. ❞
JIM CARREY

Now, if you had already put in over fifteen hours of writing and you'd again been told that your writing was bad, what would you do? (A) Tell your mentor that she wouldn't know a masterpiece if it hit her in the face. (B) Break down crying and beg her not to tell anyone that you are such a bad writer. (C) Suffer the embarrassment again in hopes of getting it right. If you were stubborn and answered (C), then you'd probably get the same results I did. She called my fourth draft "great" and told me I could be a talented writer. From that experience I learned that before you can walk you have to crawl.

When things seem to be going wrong, you can also think about this story, which has been attributed to both ancient China and India. A villager went to the local wise man for help because his horse had run away and it was time for harvesting. In response to the villager's distress, the wise man said, "Who can tell if it's good or bad?" The disgruntled villager went home only to find that his horse had returned and brought a mare with him. Now the man had two horses to help him with the harvesting. "Who can tell if it's good or bad?" said the wise man. The villager left but came back the next day because his son, his only helper, broke his leg while trying to work with the new mare. What was the farmer to do without a helper? "Who can tell if it's good or bad?" said the wise man. The villager was beginning to lose respect for the wise man so he left. But he came back once again the very next day, happy. The king's soldiers had swept through the area, drafting every able-bodied lad for battle, but because the farmer's son had a broken leg, he was spared. "Who can tell if it's good or bad?"

Remember, you are only human and cannot be expected to know all the answers all the time. However, remembering the rules on the following page might get you through some tough times.

The Rules for Being Human

1. **You will receive a body.** You may like it or hate it, but it will be yours for the entire period this time around.

2. **You will learn lessons.** You are enrolled in a full-time, informal school called life. Each day in this school you will have the opportunity to learn lessons. You may like the lessons or think them irrelevant and stupid.

3. **There are no mistakes, only lessons.** Growth is a process of trial and error, experimentation. The "failed" experiments are as much a part of the process as the experiment that ultimately "works."

4. **A lesson is repeated until it is learned.** A lesson will be presented to you in various forms until you have learned it. When you have learned it you can go on to the next lesson.

5. **Learning lessons does not end.** There is no part of life that does not contain its lessons. If you are alive, there are lessons to be learned.

6. **"There" is no better than "here."** When your "there" has become a "here," you will simply obtain another "there" that will, again, look better than "here."

7. **Others are merely mirrors of you.** You cannot love or hate something about another person unless it reflects to you something you love or hate about yourself.

8. **What you make of your life is up to you.** You have all the tools and resources you need; what you do with them is up to you. The choice is yours.

9. **The answers lie inside you.** The answers to life's questions lie inside you. All you need to do is look, listen, and trust.

10. **YOU WILL FORGET ALL THIS.**

AUTHOR UNKNOWN

> ❝ Sometimes our ideas work very well and sometimes they work very poorly. As long as we stay in the feedback loop and keep trying, it's a lot of fun. ❞
> BILL GATES

> ❝ When one door closes another door opens; but we so often look so long and so regretfully upon the closed door, that we do not see the ones which open for us. ❞
> ALEXANDER GRAHAM BELL

> ❝ I've missed three thousand shots. Twenty-six times the game-winning shot has been entrusted to me, and I've missed. I've lost over three hundred games. I've failed over and over and over again, and that is why I've succeeded. ❞
> MICHAEL JORDAN

CHAPTER 28

PAY YOURSELF 10 PERCENT FIRST AND ALWAYS

First we make our habits, then our habits make us.

DENIS WAITLEY

MUST READ:

I strongly recommend
two books to start
you down your path to
financial education: *The
Wealthy Barber* by David
Chilton (Stoddart, 2002)
and *Rich Dad, Poor
Dad* by Robert Kiyosaki
(Warner Books, 2002).

Four years after graduating, while I was running around my neighbor-hood track, I met Frank Batmale, a fifty-three-year-old firefighter. We got to talking and Frank said to me, "A guy at your age could be very wealthy by my age if you started saving a little money every year." He went on to say, "I've been saving a lot of money since my early forties, but with investing, time is more important than the amount of money you put away. If I had known to start at your age, I'd be a rich, rich man."

I wanted to know more, so Frank kindly gave me a book called *The Richest Man in Babylon* by George S. Clason (New American Library). The first chapter of this tiny best-selling book changed my life. It made me realize that since the day I started working—even during college—I've had a river of gold flowing through my hands but never kept any for myself. That river was made up of my paychecks. So I began writing my savings account a check for 10 percent of what I earned, before I did anything else with the money. Pay myself first—I liked that idea! After all, I was the one who earned the money, did the work, and put in the hours. And it seemed like a surefire way to build up a big savings, much better than paying all my bills first and hoping I had some left over (because I never had "leftover money"). The strange part was that it didn't seem as if I had any less money to spend. The great part is that 10 percent of every paycheck I earn is now mine for keeps.

Before you do anything with your take-home pay, write yourself a check first. Think about the total amount of money you've earned in your lifetime and then think about how much you've kept for yourself.

There are a lot of great reasons to sock 10 percent away. First of all, it's money that benefits you 100 percent. It doesn't go to bill collectors—it goes only to you. Second, because it will be money that you completely control, you can invest in anything you want. Nobody will be able to tell you what you have to do with that money. Third, because of the financial freedom it earns you, if you consistently save 10 percent of your earnings, eventually you'll have so much money you won't have to depend on anyone else for a paycheck!

How will the meager 10 percent you save make you rich? A giant fortune begins with only a little money (as long you invest it in something that's earning interest). Check this scenario out: Let's say you start saving when you're twenty and save $2,000 per year for five years. If you quit saving when you're twenty-five and let the money earn 12 percent interest in a tax-deferred investment until you're sixty-four, through the power of compounding interest your savings will grow to over $1 million! That's more than a 1,000 percent return on your investment! Even if you don't intend to keep the savings for that long, the money you save goes to work creating more money!

Before you jump to the conclusion that it would be impossible to save $2,000 per year for five years, consider this: All you have to earn to save $2,000 a year is $20,000 a year. I know 99 percent of those in college don't earn anywhere near that much, but when you graduate you probably will. And start the minute you read this, because time is the all-important factor in obtaining wealth through the power of compounding interest.

If you delay and don't start until you're thirty-five, there's almost no way you can catch up—even if you save $2,000 every year from thirty-five to sixty-four years old, you'll only end up with less than $500,000. The earlier you start saving, the more you'll make. And if the payback times I'm mentioning seem like forever, maybe the following example will make you feel better:

If, when you were one year old, you had sold all your baby belongings and put $1,000 into savings, you'd have $6,130 by the time you were sixteen, $10,803 on your twenty-first birthday, $19,040 at twenty-six, and $59,000 at thirty-six years old. And $1.5 million by the time you hit sixty-four! And that's just with one payment! Thirty-five years seems as if it will never arrive, but all of a sudden, there you are.

It's easy to think that there are many months when you can't afford to pay yourself 10 percent. But ask yourself this: How often do you call

44 When you get there, there is no there there. But there will be a pool. **77**
DAVID ZUCKER, *director*

44 The most powerful force in the universe is compound interest. **77**
ALBERT EINSTEIN

HOT TIP: *Getting Loaded: 50 Start Now Strategies for Making 1,000,000 While You're Still Young Enough to Enjoy It* by Peter Bielagus. Also check out his website at www.peterbspeaks.com.

44 I found the road to wealth when I decided that a part of all I earn was mine to keep. **77**
GEORGE S. CLASON, *author*

**   If you don't look ahead, nobody will—there's no time to kill. **
CLINT BLACK, *singer*

HOT TIP: Studies have estimated that for every one hundred people in the United States, at retirement age thirty-six will be dead, thirty-six will be broke, five will still be working, four will be retired, and one will have financial freedom.

your boss and say, "This has been a particularly tough month and I can't afford to pay my Social Security tax, my FICA tax, and my state tax—please don't deduct them this month." You could say that to your boss but he'd treat you as if you were crazy. Taxes have to be paid no matter what. That's why Dr. David Schwartz, author of *The Magic of Thinking Success* (Wilshire Book Co., 1987), suggests you call your 10 percent self-payment a Financial Freedom Tax. He says, "To reap the benefits of your hard work and pull yourself out of economic slavery, you must pay your FFT just as you pay the other taxes. Remember, the FFT is the only tax you'll ever pay that goes to work for you and those you love. All other taxes are paid to people you don't know for purposes you may or may not approve of."

One other thing—paying yourself 10 percent first will be a heck of a lot easier if you don't buy items that lose value over time—like new cars. Did you know the moment you drive a new car off the lot it loses a huge chunk of its value? Yes-siree! On average, new automobiles lose more than 20 percent of their value in their first year. Not buying something expensive that's going to lose one-fifth of its value can make a huge difference in your bankroll. For example, imagine that you have $20,000 of extra money after one year of working full-time and you decide you need to buy a car. Instead of spending $15,000 on a new car, and losing $3,000 of value in the first year, let's say you decide to shop around for a cool used convertible—and get one for $8,000. Your first big benefit is that your convertible will probably be worth $7,000 by the year's end, figuring you don't drive into any telephone poles. Your further good fortune is that you still have $12,000 to invest instead of the $5,000 you'd have had you bought new. (Let's not forget car insurance and registration is a lot more expensive for new cars.) Let that $12,000 grow at an average of 15 percent per year and you'll have over $48,500 in ten years. Not bad at all—especially compared to the many new car buyers you'll know who still don't get more dates and who have a whole heck of a lot less money in the bank. Leave that money in the bank for another ten years and it becomes about $200,000!

P.S.—Did I mention that Sam Walton, founder of Wal-Mart, drove a used pickup till the day he died? Um, you think his spending habits had anything to do with the wealth he accumulated?

CHAPTER 29

BE GOOD TO OTHERS

There are two ways of exerting one's strength; one is pushing down, the other is pulling up.

BOOKER T. WASHINGTON

At this point in the book, you've read about several fundamentals of success: the ability to focus on what you care about; the ability to make bold decisions; the desire to commit yourself to taking the time to make your dreams come true; the courage to break through your failures; the good sense to pay yourself 10 percent, first and always. Nonetheless, you can put focus, commitment, boldness, persistence, and even money to work for you and not end up successful if you don't make people around you feel good about themselves.

Numerous writers have told the story of an ancient but nearly forgotten Christian monastery. No new monks had joined in years, and one by one the elderly ones were dying off. Eventually only five aged monks were left, and the monastic order seemed near extinction. Then one day, while one of the monks was walking in the nearby forest, he encountered an equally aged wise-looking rabbi. He explained the situation to the rabbi and asked him if he had any advice. The rabbi replied with great seriousness and certainty, "I can't give you any advice, but I can tell you this: One of you five monks is the Messiah."

Stunned, the monk returned to his monastery and passed this news on to the others. At first everyone was shocked, but slowly they became more and more accustomed to the idea, and eventually, whenever they would encounter one another, each would think, "Perhaps he's the Messiah." But there wasn't any way to actually determine which one of them was the Messiah, and none of them really felt that he was the one. So they all began to act as if any of them might be the Messiah—treating each other with great love, compassion, and respect. As a result, things

> 66 Happiness is a perfume you cannot pour on others without getting a few drops on yourself. 99
> OG MANDINO, *author*

> 66 May I never get too busy in my own affairs that I fail to respond to the needs of others with kindness and compassion. 99
> THOMAS JEFFERSON

began to change. People who passed through were impressed by the love and respect that radiated from each of the monks. Word about the monastery spread, and younger men came to investigate. Soon the monastery was thriving again and the tradition continued with renewed spirit and energy.

In many ways, we're all pretty much the same when it comes to our aspirations. We all want to feel likable, important, and good about the things we do. Nothing feels better than meeting someone who recognizes our importance, accomplishments, and good qualities. Think about the people you would do anything for—aren't they people that like, praise, or admire you? A brief piece by an anonymous author may help you keep in mind the impact other people have had in your life, and the impact you can have on theirs.

> *Do you remember who gave you your first break? Someone saw something in you once. That's partly why you are where you are today. It could have been a thoughtful parent, a perceptive teacher, a demanding drill sergeant, an appreciative employer, or just a friend who dug down in his pocket and came up with a few bucks. Whoever it was had the kindness and the foresight to bet on your future. These are two beautiful qualities that separate the human being from the orangutan. In the next twenty-four hours, take ten minutes to write a grateful note to the person who helped you. You'll keep a wonderful friendship alive. Matter of fact, take another ten minutes to give somebody else a break. Who knows? Someday you might get a nice letter. It could be one of the most gratifying messages you ever read.*

If you want help while you move toward your goals, help the people around you move toward theirs first. If you want compliments for the things you accomplish or the traits you possess, first give the people around you compliments that they deserve. If you want people to notice your gifts, first notice theirs. If you want to benefit from other people's expertise, give other people the benefit of yours. The point is people will treat you as well as you treat them.

One summer, I worked with a college student named Randy, who was actively pursuing his dream job. At only twenty he was already focused on what he cared about, committed to putting in lots of extra effort, overcoming mistakes, and even making bold decisions. But when it came to helping the other college students we were working with, Randy was unavailable. He kept everything he knew to himself in hopes of

" We are here on earth to do good to others. What the others are here for, I don't know. **"**
W. H. AUDEN, *poet and essayist*

" Many of the things you can count don't count. Many of the things you can't count, really count. **"**
ALBERT EINSTEIN

" What you remember, what you measure yourself by, what you cling to as you get older is what you have done as a family, what you have done for others, your own naked humanity. **"**
BARBARA BUSH, *former first lady*

having a competitive advantage. The most shocking instance was when he flatly refused to tell another student how to get a VIP to go to lunch with you—something Randy knew very well how to do. He paid a high price to keep what he felt were his "competitive secrets." By the end of the summer, all the other team members, including myself, had isolated him, and he confided in me that the situation caused him great stress and disappointment. What goes around, comes around.

Too many people believe that if you give away good advice, you give away your secret recipe. And that if you give someone a great compliment, you suddenly become a lesser person. Both assumptions are false! You could give away all the good advice you have and still not have given away your competitive edge because your competitive edge is you—your unique blend of personality, talent, and experience. You could give the highest compliments in the world without ever implying that you are any less.

Are you in the habit of giving compliments? There's a lot of ways to get started. Compliment people about their appearance, about their ideas, accomplishments, family, or interests; about their material possessions, their name, the way they answer a phone; about their smile, the way they speak; how well they listen; or even about how nicely they compliment you! Compliment people on anything you genuinely like. (The key is to be genuine.) No matter how far you go or how much you excel, never forget that each person you meet does something that is worthy of your admiration. Treat everyone with the same respect and attention you hope they'll give you, and you will greatly increase your chances of being greeted by smiles and helping hands.

When I was growing up, my mother would often say, "Always take time to make people around you feel good about themselves—your attention can change a person's life and it leaves you feeling wonderful." One of my college roommates told me I had a gift for sharing my enthusiasm with others. That single, positive comment gave me a deep-seated belief that I could someday use this gift to help others.

My story pales in comparison to the true life story of Carl Lewis, the most successful track-and-field star in history, who won nine Olympic gold medals. As a kid his destiny was deeply affected by four simple words. When Carl was a kid, his parents took him to meet track legend Jesse Owens. "He said three things, and I took it as encouragement, and it lasted for a long time. Can you believe it? He said three or four words, and look what an effect it had on me. Owens didn't even know

> **" Whoever renders service to many puts himself/herself in line for greatness—great wealth, great return, great satisfaction, great reputation, and great joy. "**
> JIM ROHN, *motivational speaker and entrepreneur*

> **" No one will ever love you for your work or accomplishments. People will love you for the way you make them feel. "**
> NANCY COMBS, *my mom*

> **" If you help others, you will be helped, perhaps tomorrow, perhaps in one hundred years, but you will be helped. Nature must pay off the debt. . . . It is a mathematical law and all life is mathematics. "**
> G. I. GURDJIEFF, *philosopher*

me personally. He was encouraging a little kid. He said, 'You could be good,' and I believed it. I totally did."

A friend of mine, Christian Haren, has used his gifts to help others, and in doing so has expanded my understanding about the power of treating people well. Christian has led an almost mythical existence. In his lifetime, he's been a marine, a top male model, an actor both on screen and stage; he's written a screenplay, owned and lived on a ranch, and attended some top-notch universities. He is also one of the longest surviving people afflicted with AIDS.

After being diagnosed with AIDS twelve years ago, Christian was told that he only had a short time to live. However, he has not only survived, but for the past eleven years, he's been reaching out to thousands of youths, parents, and educators across the country as a teacher of AIDS awareness. Almost daily, Christian is giving love, joy, and hope to people he's never met, and he gets an abundance back in return. After years of loneliness, in spite of his fortune and fame, he says, "Finally I'm in the process of joining the human race." What has kept him going? Christian has a guess: "I think all the love and joy I've gotten from people over the past twelve years has kept me alive for so long."

There is no scarcity when it comes to smart advice, genuine compliments, or good old-fashioned loving actions—so use all of them to make other people feel better about themselves. Nothing will make you feel better on the inside, and nothing will bring you more true love and affection. Honestly, who doesn't like love and affection?

Let me end this chapter with a brief piece by Ralph Waldo Emerson.

Success

To laugh often and much;
To win the respect of intelligent people
and the affection of children;
To earn the appreciation of honest critics
and endure the betrayal of false friends;
To appreciate beauty;
To find the best in others;
To leave the world a bit better, whether by a healthy child, a garden
patch or a redeemed social condition;
To know even one life has breathed easier because you
have lived;
This is to have succeeded.

66 Too often we underestimate the power of a touch, a smile, a kind word, a listening ear, or the smallest act of caring, all of which have the potential to turn a life around. **99**
LEO BUSCAGLIA,
professor and author

66 You have not lived a perfect day unless you've done something for someone who will never be able to repay you. **99**
RUTH SMELTZER, *author*

66 When you extend yourself in kindness and spirit, one to another, that comes back to you. **99**
OPRAH WINFREY

CHAPTER 30

BON VOYAGE!

There is no better time than right after graduation to be terribly idealistic, uncompromising, and gutsy. My advice is simple: Go for it. Life is not a game to be won; it is a game to be played. To the players go the game.

DONALD ASHER

It has been many years since I wrote *Major in Success*, and this revised edition offers me an opportunity to share more advice with you. The biggest thing I've learned since writing it is that it's all about action. If you want extraordinary things to happen in your life, then put the suggested steps into action. Don't delay. Don't question whether they'll work for you. Just take action. Success isn't rocket science—it is a fantastic hike that you go on by moving your feet. I feel enormously fortunate to have been able to become a professional speaker, and I know that I got here primarily by taking the action steps and committing to the six habits suggested in this book.

So how does this relate to you? Well, you've now considered your interests, passions, and aspirations. You've brainstormed future job possibilities that match who you truly are. You've begun to disarm some of your fears. You've started doing the activities that make you very valuable in the working world. And you've learned the habits that create success. Now treat yourself to a few thoughts about what is possible for you.

Never underestimate what you can do during college. College students have launched almost every kind of business under the sun, from health food stores to clothing companies. College students have starred in movies and commercials, written best-selling books, published groundbreaking research, shot photos for national publications, launched successful record labels, and on and on. The majority of students will just

> ❝ You know what I think was the one great thing I did? I went for it. I think that's the only thing I've done that was great. ❞
> JON STEWART

> ❝ We're all worms. But I do believe that I am a glowworm. ❞
> WINSTON CHURCHILL

173

study, test, study, and test. But some people, possibly yourself included, will add to the list of incredible things college students have done—and it won't be a miracle or luck or good fortune. It will happen because a student went for it.

- College students launched Microsoft.
- College students made the smash-hit film *The Blair Witch Project*.
- College students revolutionized the world by programming the first Web browser, Mosaic (which was the precursor to Netscape Navigator).
- College students have written hit movies such as *Good Will Hunting* and *Boyz n the Hood*.
- A college student started Kinko's at his local university.
- A college student started FedEx.
- A college student wrote a report that landed her on *Larry King Live*, earned her a six-figure publishing deal, and affected the U.S. Senate.
- A college student launched Dell Computers.
- A college student booked Bill Cosby to speak at an event for thousands.
- A college student discovered the band Live and managed them to many #1 hits.
- A college student launched the nationwide nonprofit organization Teach for America.
- College students have created some of the most popular Internet sites in the world, including Yahoo!, theGlobe, and CollegeClub.
- A college student launched the city newspaper in Madison, Connecticut.
- A college student launched Aardvark Studios, which shoots photos of millions of graduating high school seniors.

When someone knows what they want out of life, knows that there are many ways to turn their passions into a career, and when someone is motivated by dreams, they truly have most of what it takes to turn their dreams into reality.

Maybe you're smart, maybe you're not—who cares? Maybe you came from a wealthy and supportive background, maybe you didn't—who cares? Maybe you're motivated by a lot of things, maybe by a few. It doesn't matter. What matters is focusing on what motivates you most and giving your dreams a chance. Still not convinced that it's possible to allow your dreams to live? Then pay careful attention to the following ten statements because they're not just words, they're secrets that many people have discovered and used to realize their dreams.

Top Ten Reasons You Can Get Your Dream Job

10. Ordinary people do extraordinary things.

9. People who achieve success rarely know how they'll accomplish it (they only believe it is possible).

8. You don't have to be twice as good as everyone else—just a little bit better.

7. "The secret of success is constancy of purpose." —Benjamin Disraeli

6. "The world stands aside to let anyone pass who knows where he or she is going." —David Starr Jordon

5. "Nothing will take you farther than persistence." —Calvin Coolidge

4. "Anything can be achieved by taking action, deciding what's working and what's not, and changing the approach until you achieve what you want." —Anthony Robbins

3. "Luck favors the person who is going after their dreams." —Richard Nelson Bolles

2. "That the moment one definitely commits oneself then Providence moves too. All sorts of things occur to help one that would never otherwise have occurred." —W. H. Murray

1. If at first you don't succeed, you're like everyone else who went on to greatness.

While I know many people who would testify to the truth of the ten reasons above, the best thing to do is confirm them for yourself. Try them out. Put them to work for you. Anything is possible if you just make a decision to take action and try your best.

> It's time to stop tiptoeing around the pool and jump into the deep end, head first. It's time to think big, want more, and achieve it all!
> MARK VICTOR HANSEN, author and motivational speaker

> Nothing is as real as a dream. The world can change around you, but your dream will not. Responsibilities need not erase it. Duties need not obscure it. Because the dream is within you, no one can take it away.
> TOM CLANCY, *author*

True power and extraordinary results

When I was writing this book, I knew the steps I was suggesting worked,
but now I understand that their power to create extraordinary results
cannot be underestimated. Since I began following through on the action steps and truly committed to the six habits, my career has taken off
and I constantly feel like shouting, "I did it! I did it! I did it!" I actually
carved out a career for myself doing something I truly enjoy, truly am
grateful to do, and wouldn't trade it for the world. The best part is that
the rewards keep getting bigger and bigger.

In one of my all-time favorite books, *The Alchemist*, author Paulo
Coelho teaches that everyone on Earth has a treasure that awaits them,
and that, "When you're searching for your treasure, you'll discover things
along the way you'd never have discovered had you not had the courage
to try for things that seemed impossible for you." Begin searching for
your treasure now. Dream big. Take action. Develop successful habits,
and be great. Becoming successful is easier than most people make it out
to be, and dreams really do come true.

Go for it—you've got what it takes!

BONUS APPENDIX

Bonus Tips for Teachers, Artists, Exchange Students, and Athletes

Teachers

Everything in *Major in Success* applies to those who want to be teachers, and in particular, you'll benefit from knowing these five things: First, two teaching credentials make you twice as valuable. Second, if you've been involved in a campus club or in a sport, you will be much more likely to be hired because you're more valuable if you can help run student activities or coach a sport. Third, computers are everywhere in schools, so being good with computers is essential. Fourth, being bilingual is so helpful to teachers. And finally, the right extracurriculars, such as working in a daycare center, being involved with kids through your church, running a Girl Scouts' club, demonstrate to a school administrator that you truly enjoy working with kids.

Hot Tip for Teachers

Call (614) 485-1111 to get a copy of *The Job Search Handbook for Educators* if you're going into the K–12 environment. If you're going to teach in higher education, you want *The Higher Education Job Search* (http://aaee.org).

Artists

This book was written with you very much in mind, especially since artists are aiming for very cool jobs. Add these five philosophies to your approach to success: First, the biggest mistake most art students make after graduating is they come up with noncreative solutions to the pragmatic problem of survival, like waiting tables fifty hours a week so they can afford to live in New York City. Noncreative solutions like this will drain your creative spirit. You will have a much better and more rewarding life if you solve your challenges of survival creatively, like living in New Jersey where the rent is much less and commuting into New York City. Teaching kids to finger paint for part-time work is more creative than waiting tables. Second, don't stay on the fence trying to decide whether you'll stick with the arts or not. The indecision is a big waste of energy.

Simply decide to commit to it for five years. You'll be amazed at how this frees up your mind to think creatively. Third, stay in touch with friends in the arts. You'll meet other artists in school and after school. Cultivate these relationships. Be a great networker. Artists often rise together. Artists you know will succeed and need a director for their play, need to fill a gallery space, need to recommend another actor. If you've cultivated these relationships, your lucky breaks will come much more often. Fourth, create a lifestyle with the lowest money needs possible. This will take a lot of pressure off. And finally, the arts, although often restrictive in money and security, have so much to offer for people who truly value creativity and individuality. So, in the words of Jim Petosa, artistic director of the Olney Theatre in Washington, D.C., "If you're not going to enjoy the tremendous liberated feeling afforded by being in the arts, then don't do it."

Hot Tips for Artists

Check out these books:

> *Careers for Music Lovers & Other Tuneful Types* (VGM Publishing)
> *Opportunities in Performing Arts Careers* (VGM Publishing)
> *Opportunities in Visual Arts Careers* (VGM Publishing)
> *The Working Actors Guide to Los Angeles* (Aaron Blake Publishing), 800-729-6423

These websites:

- www.artspresenters.org (key organization for any performing artist or theater manager)
- http://artjob.org (great source for jobs in the visual arts)
- http://westaf.org (awesome source of links for visual artists and independent filmmakers)
- www.nyfa.org (online community for the arts, great for links and connections in the art world)

Athletes

The question I get most often from athletes is, "How can I fit in things like a semester overseas, campus clubs, and internships? Sports take up all my free time." I answer with a story.

An exceptional college athlete I met, Ben Wittowski, ran track year-round, devoting at least twenty hours to sports every week. He also fit in a twenty-hour-a-week internship, during three different semesters—one with a sports agent, one promoting his school's Midnight Madness event, and another for a professor, helping to promote the university's baseball games. His grades were excellent during these busy times. However, interestingly, his grades went down the semester he did only school and track. He told me it left him with too much time on his hands and his time management suffered all around. There is research to back up what Ben discovered on his own. Studies have confirmed that with a lot to do, people use their time well and do better in all their activities. People with extra time, on the other hand, feel less urgency and end up squandering valuable time. Their performance suffers as a result. The second question I get from athletes is, "If I don't make it as a professional athlete, what should I do?" I stick with the philosophy of "follow your bliss." Consider following your passion for sports into a sports industry job. The following books will turn you on to the many job options for people with a passion for sports:

Careers for Sports Nuts & Other Athletic Types by William Ray Heitzmann

The 50 Coolest Jobs in Sports: Who's Got Them, What They Do, and How You Can Get One! by David Fischer

The Guide to Careers in Sports by Leonard Karlin

You Can't Play the Game If You Don't Know the Rules: Career Opportunities in Sports Management by David M. Carter

Career Opportunities in the Sports Industry by Shelly Field

Sports Market Place: Guide to over 10,000 Sports Organizations, Teams, Corporate Sponsors, Sports Agents, Marketing and Event Management Agencies, Media, Manufacturers and Retailers, edited by Richard Lipsey (Look for this one in your library because it sells for $199.)

http://jobsinsports.com has job listings, but also charges a monthly subscription fee

WEBSITES FOR SUCCESS

Job and Career Sites

http://backdoorjobs.com
http://careerbuilder.com
http://careermag.com
http://collegegrad.com
http://craigslist.com
http://fastcompany.com/guides/
　reinvent.html
www.internjobs.com
www.jobhuntersbible.com
http://jobstar.org
www.jobweb.com
www.monster.com
www.resortjobs.com
http://rileyguide.com
www.studentjobs.gov
www.summerjobs.com
http://sustainablebusiness.com
www.wetfeet.com

Professional Associations and Societies

www.societyofsuccess.com
www.weddles.com/associations/
　index.cfm
www.marketingsource
　.com/associations/

Patrick Combs Sites (Free Newsletter Sign-up)

www.patrickcombs.com
http://coachedbypatrick.com
http://man1bank0.com
http://myspace.com/patrickcombs

Making a Difference

http://sageworks.net (get Making
　a Difference College and
　Graduate Guide)

Volunteering

www.americaspromise.org
http://americorps.org
www.volunteermatch.org
http://servenet.org
http://strength.org

Friends of Patrick Combs

http://gotohealth.com
http://getmotivation.com
http://societyofsuccess.com
www.friendsofwfp.org
http://internprograms.com
http://eagleu.com
http://focusedstudent.com
www.totalsuccess.com

Anton Anderson Site

antonanderson.com

MORE WAYS TO MAJOR IN SUCCESS

Coaching

Patrick Combs offers students a powerful coaching program for less than $1.50 a day.

Give it a try for a month and it'll make you a believer. Give it a year, and your life will never be the same. www.coachedbypatrick.com.

Patrick's Free Newsletter

Visit Patrick's website and subscribe to his free inspirational newsletter for friends. At his site, you'll also find his blog, stories about Patrick's career, free articles on success, inspirational quotes, and much more.

- http://goodthink.com

Audiobooks, E-books, CDs, and DVDs

Patrick Combs has many motivational products in his online store. To browse or order, visit Patrick's store at http://goodthink.com.

Speeches

Patrick Combs is one of the college circuit's most popular speakers. You, as a student, have the power to help bring him to your school. To learn more about how you can influence your college or university to have Patrick come speak, contact the Good Thinking Co., at (619) 291-4743, or visit http://goodthink.com.

Do Other Students a Favor

If you have some good words to say about *Major in Success*, please post your review of the book at www.amazon.com and www.bn.com. You'll be helping more students turn on to this book.

ABOUT THE AUTHOR

College Attended: Lewis & Clark College for a year and a half, then went on to graduate from San Francisco State University.

What I Really Do: I have a triple life as an inspirational speaker (http://goodthink.com), a comedic theater performer (http://man1bank0.com), and a success coach (http://coachedbypatrick.com). It has me passionate, traveling, making people laugh, making a difference, and loving life.

What I Did Before: Couple of summers before writing this book I was a video game tester. Before that, for two years, I was producer of a highly acclaimed multimedia event about leadership called *A Day in the Future*. My first job out of college was at Levi Strauss & Co., first as an intern and then later as videoconferencing manager. During college I managed a great rock band called the Square Roots.

Most Loved Movie Experience: *Defending Your Life* by Albert Brooks (No Fear!), *The Matrix*, and *Lord of the Rings*!

Dreams and Ambitions: Being the best inspirational speaker I can be; rocking HBO with my one-man show; writing a book that changes a million lives; creating the largest and greatest coaching program in the world; having my own foundation and giving away millions; and seeing the world in an adventurous way.

My Heroes: Bono, Will Rogers, Muhammad Ali, my mom.

Blast from the Past: Outward Bound for twenty-one days in the desert. Check it out: http://goodthink.com in the stories section.

What I Think Life Is All About: Expansion and love. Take that!

ABOUT THE VIP CONTRIBUTOR

College Attended: Mira Costa Community College for two and a half years, studied abroad in Australia for half a year, then transferred to University of California at Santa Barbara and graduated with a BA in communication.

What Do I Do?: I am an aspiring speaker, writer, consultant, real-estate investor, and success coach.

Why Do I Do It?: I love the freedom and excitement of my career path and also the opportunity to help others break through their personal barriers.

What I Did Before: In college I had two great internships with companies that I would recommend any student check out: The National Society of Leadership and Success and The Power of Focus. After graduation I took a four-month trip around the United Kingdom and Europe with my fiancé. I would recommend everyone find a way to travel before they start working.

What I Think Life Is All About: Joy, love, health, abundance, and laughter.

INDEX

A

Ackerman, Diane, 99
action, importance of taking, 173
Adams, Charles Kendall, 100
Adams Electronic Job Search Almanac 2000 (Blackett), 143
Aguilera, 43
The Alchemist (Coelho), 176
Ali, Muhammad, 49, 68
Allen, James, 176
Allen, Jeffrey, 4
Allen, Marcus, 40, 41
Allen, Woody, 27, 128
Altshuler, Michael, 75
Anderson, Anton, 79–81, 88
Andretti, Mario, 147
artists, bonus tips for, 177–178
Asher, Donald, 90, 92, 173
athletes, bonus tips for, 178–179
Auden, W. H., 170
Awaken the Giant Within (Robbins), 151

B

Bach, Richard, 162
Baldwin, James, 26
Ball, Lucille, 43
Barrymore, Drew, 6
Barrymore, John, 26
Baruch, Bernard, 135
Bates, Michael, 61–62, 63, 65, 151
Batmale, Frank, 166
beating the system, 153–154
beer, jobs for people who like, 19
The Beer Log (Robertson), 19
Before They Were Famous (Waitley), 10
Bell, Alexander Graham, 151, 165
Bell, Confucius, 90
Beneteau, Rick, 31
Berra, Yogi, 8
Better Grades in Less Time (Tuerack), 64
Black, Clint, 168
Black, H. Duane, 164
Black Monday phenomena, 5
bliss, following, 26
Bloom, Benjamin, 3
Blum, Arlene, 41
The Body Shop, 16
Bok, Derek, 66

Bolles, Richard, 144, 175
Borden, Win, 74
Bourne, Alec, 16
Brassington, Duncan, 38
Bristol, Claude M., 152
Brock, Peter, 57
Brooks, Garth, 8
Brown, Jr., H. Jackson , 74
Buddah, 42
Buffett, Jimmy, 26
bungee-jumping, 16, 45
Bureau of Labor Statistics, 141–142
Buscaglia, Leo, 172
Bush, Barbara, 170
Bushwell, Nolan, 37
Buss, Trevver, 52, 53
Butler, Edward B., 37

C

Caleb, Charles, 27
Campbell, Joseph, 26, 143
campus clubs, 58–59, 60. *See also* extracurricular activities
Campus Connections magazine, 74
Cape Winelands District Municipality, 150
Captain Picard, 140
Caracciolo, Derek, 65
career books, 19–20
career choice. *See* naysayers
career options, 140
CareerXroads 2003 (Mehler and Crispin), 143
Carey, Mariah, 43
Carnegie, Dale, 125
Carrey, Jim, 18, 26, 41, 63, 163
Carson, Johnny, 43, 127, 162
Carter-Scott, Cherie, 157
Carver, Roberta, 118
Chambers, Veronica, 88, 94–96, 151, 159
Cheetham, Sophie, 149–151
Chicken Soup for the Soul (Canfield/Hansen), 163
Childre, Doc, 81
Chilton, David, 166
Chung, Connie, 119
Churchill, Winston, 173, 174

Clancy, Tom, 175
Clapton, Eric, 24
Clason, George S., 166, 167
Clemenceau, Georges, 164
Clinton, Bill, 119
co-ops, 118. *See also* internships
coaching, 86–89
Coehlo, Paulo, 41, 176
college major
    impact on career choice, 16, 44
    narrowness/broadness of, 17
Collins, Nancy, 119
Colton, Charles Caleb, 155
Combs, Nancy, 171
Combs, Sean (P-Diddy), 24
company guides, 20
compass, built-in, 12–13
competition, 45–46
compliments, 171
conferences, 108
Confucius, 19, 39
Conlon, Jim, 44
Coolidge, Calvin, 85, 113, 175
Corgan, Billy, 30
Council on International Educational Exchange (CIEE), 53–54
Couric, Katie, 163
Covey, Stephen, 75, 76
credit cards
    benefits of, 130–131
    credit reporting services, 132
    establishing credit through, 129
    "freeloading," 129
    guidelines for using, 131–132, 134
    how to choose, 134–135
    teaser rates, 135
CreditAbility, 132–133
Critical Path (Fuller), 156
Crotty, James, 18
Crowe, Sheryl, 24
Cryer, Bruce, 81
Csikszentimihalyi, Mihaly, 11, 152

D

Davenport, Rita, 27
De Bono, Edward, 144
debit cards, 130

Delacroix, Eugene, 105
Dikel, Margaret F., 140
Dini, R. C., 29
Dion, Celine, 24
Disney, Walt, 4
Disraeli, Benjamin, 175
Do It! Let's Get off Our Butts
    (McWilliams), 153
doing what you love, benefits of, 6–7
Duchovny, David, 10, 11
Dyer, Wayne, 28
Dylan, Bob, 44

E
Earnhardt, Dale, 164
Ebert, Roger, 45, 161
Edison, Thomas, 5, 59, 162
Eggers, Dave, 55–57, 119, 151, 152
Einstein, Albert, 14, 34, 167, 170
"Ekin" department, 142
Electronic Entertainment magazine, 19
electronic job searching, 141–142
*Electronic Resumes and Online
    Networking* (Smith), 143
embarrassment, lessening, 43
Emerson, Ralph Waldo, 4, 24, 156, 172
Engelbart, Doug, 43, 162
enthusiasm factor, 45
Entrepreneur Media Inc., 142
Equifax Information Service, 132
Ewing, Patrick, 119
Experien!, 132
extracurricular activities, 56, 57–58, 59
Eyre, Richard, 137

F
faith, replacing fear with, 42–46
Faludi, Susan, 23
fear of success, 8–9
fears
    five prescriptions for, 40–53
    six big, 39–40
50 Cent, 24
Figler, Howard, 44, 142
financial freedom. *See* savings
financial stability, establishing, 130
Finesilver, Sherman, 31, 88
First Things First (Covey/Merrill/
    Merrill), 75
fitness, jobs for people who like, 19
FM 2030, 98
Forbes, Malcolm S., 78

Ford, Henry, 45
Foster, Oscar, 49
Foundation for Student
    Communications, 101
Franklin, Benjamin, 145
Franssen, Margot, 16, 17
"freeloading," 130
Frieberg, Jerome, 96
frugality, 167–168
Fuller, R. Buckminster, 156, 162, 163

G
Gallagher, 66
Gandhi, Mahatma, 45, 114
Gates, Bill, 3, 13, 56, 156, 160, 165
Georno, Jean, 159
Gerber, H. Joseph, 159
Get a Financial Life (Kobliner), 136
The Gift of Giving (Lynberg), 26–27
Gilbert, A.C., 3
goals, committing yourself to, 161
Goethe, 47
Goodall, Jane, 31
G.P.A. *See* grades
Gracian, Baltasar, 75
grades
    importance of, 62–67
    truths about grades, 66–67
Graham, Martha, 31
The Greatest Salesman in the World, 43
greatness, denominators of, 3–4
Green, David, 90–91
Greenleaf, Robert K., 81
Gretzky, Wayne, 5
Gurdjieff, G. I., 171

H
Handey, Jack, 30
Hanks, Tom, 10
Hansen, Mark Victor, 175
Haren, Christian, 172
Harris, Sydney J., 24
*A Heartbreaking Work of Staggering
    Genius* (Eggers), 55
Hendricks, Howard, 153
Hilfiger, Tommy, 89
Hill, Napoleon, 33, 40
Hillary, Sir Edmund, 121
HIV/AIDS pandemic, 149
Holton, Ed, 142
How to Sell Yourself (Girard), 72

*How to Win Friends and Influence
    People* (Carnegie), 125
Hughes, Keven, 152
human relations/interpersonal
    communications course, 71

I
*I Could do Anything If I Only Knew What
    It Was* (Sher and Smith), 15
Iacocca, Lee, 128
*If You Want to Be Rich & Happy Don't
    Go to School* (Chilton), 45
Industrial Light and Magic , 128–129
information resources, 96–98
informational interviewing, 90–93, 103
Interactive Records, 90
internship course, 70–71
internships
    in Africa, 150
    defined, 117–118
    obtaining, 93, 119
    value of, 17
    what to expect, 120
interview don'ts, 126
interview do's, 125
interview plan, 122–126
interviews
    appropriate dress for, 124
    follow-ups and thank yous, 126
    good human relations principles
        and, 125
    investigate the company, 123–124
    practice at the career center, 125
    research for, 123
    resume and cover letters, 124
    show-and-tell items, 124

J
Jackson, Jesse, 122
Jackson, Michael, 24
Jam Master Jay, 24
Jefferson, Thomas, 109, 169
Jennings, Peter, 21
Job Bank USA website, 141
job changing, 16
*Job Hunter's Sourcebook: Where to
    Find Employment Leads and
    Other Job Search Resources*
    (Swartout), 20, 139
job idea generator, 21–22
job information websites, 19
job satisfaction, 4

job statistics, 22
Jobs, Steve, 137
Jordan, David Starr, 175
Jordan, Michael, 100, 160, 164, 165, 176
journaling
    benefits of, 35–37
    tips on, 34–35
    values definition, 34
    why it works, 32–33
Jung, Carl, 34

K

Kehoe, John, 102
Keller, Helen, 86, 157
Kennedy, Leo, 77
Khrushchev, Nikita, 11
Kimeldorf, Martin, 105
King, Basil, 156
King, Jr., Martin Luther , 34, 150
King, Larry, 33
Kingsley, Charles, 7
the Kinks, 12, 32, 34
Kiyosaki, Robert, 44–45, 166
Klein, Calvin, 119
Kobliner, Beth, 136
Kopp, Wendy, 101–105, 155–156
Kulwicki, Alan, 45

L

Lamb, Karen, 77
Lamu, Adamu, 27
Lane, Michael, 18
language course, 72
Lauengco, Maria, 52
Leach, Reggie, 94
leadership books, 84
leadership training, 79–80, 82, 84
learning, enthusiasm for, 13–14
learning style, 72–73
Leberecht, Scott, 128–129
Lee, Spike, 119
LeMonde, Greg, 160
Leno, Jay, 31, 43, 157, 162
Letterman, David, 31, 42, 119, 162
Letters to a Young Poet (Rilke), 27
Lewis, Carl, 87, 171–172
Lewis, Thereza, 126–127
Light, Richard, 74
Lincoln, Abraham, 89
Lindquist, Chris, 19
long-term outlook, importance of,
    159–161

Lord, M. G., 33
Louie, Gilman, 106–107
Lovelace, Butch, 45
Lowe, Deborah, 86–87
Luther, Martin, 42
Lynberg, Michael, 35

M

Macewan, Norman, 25
Mackay, Harvey B., 25, 45, 99, 121–122,
    161
Mackay Envelope Corp., 121
Madonna, 30
magazine list, 13
The Magic of Thinking Success
    (Schwartz), 168
Making the Most of College (Light), 74
Mallory, George, 60
Maloney, Dayle, 33
The Man Who Planted Trees (Giorno),
    159
Mandingo, Og, 169
Mansinne, Alexis, 156–157
Margolin, Malcolm, 54
marketing course, 72
Marx, Karl, 43
Maslow, Abraham, 1
Mason, John, 60
master's degree, 144–145
The Matrix, 164
May, Rollo, 157
McConaughey, Matthew, 43
McNamara, Jessica, internship
    experience, 114–116
McSweeney's magazine, 55
McWilliams, Peter, 42
mentoring. *See* coaching
Merrill, Rebecca R., 75
Midler, Bette, 5
Might magazine, 55, 56–57, 151
Miller, Lisa, 19
The Mind-Expanding, Options-
    Enhancing, Eye-Poppin' Chart
    of OTHER Jobs That Make
    Big Bank, 27–29
Minjares, Michael, 58
mistakes, making, 162–164
Mobil Corp., 103
Mollan-Masters, Renee, 72–73
Monk magazine, 18
Monroe, Marilyn, 28
Monstertrack website, 141

Mother Teresa, 174
Murchison, Jr., Clint, 28
Murray, W. H., 175

N

The National Society of Leadership and
    Success, 79
National Speakers Association, 109
naysayers, 20–21, 43–44
Needleman, Jacob, 27
*Negotiating Your Salary: How to Make
    $1000 a Minute* (Ten Speed
    Press), 142
Nehru, Jawaharial, 60
*Nice Job: The Guide to Cool, Odd, Risky,
    and Gruesome Ways to Make a
    Living,* 20
Nike, 142, 144
Nin, Anaïs, 42
Nuckols, Deborah, 23

O

O'Brien, Conan, 31, 42, 161
O'Brien, Dan, 162–163
Oh, the Places You'll Go! (Seuss), 136
Onyx, 24
organization and time management, 77
Oshman, Ken, 12
overseas experience benefits, 52–53
Ovid, 106
Owens, Jesse, 171–172

P

Parry, Matt, 24
passion
    benefit of having, 5–7
    exploring many aspects, 13–14
    importance of discovering, 11
    pursuing, 46
passion pinpointer exercise, 11
Patanjali, 149
Peale, Norman Vincent, 44
Personal Finance for Dummies (Tyson),
    136
Peter F. Drucker Foundation, 79
Peters, Tom, 3, 59, 103
Petty, Tom, 41
Phillips, Michael, 44
*Portfolio Power: The New Way to Show-
    case All Your Job Skills and Ex-
    periences* (Kimeldorf), 105
post-college travel, 145–146

priorities, focusing on, 75–76
procrastination, 77
Professioal Careers Sourcebook, 21–22
Professional Association Chart, *110–112*
professional associations, 106–107, 108
promotions/public relations courses, 69

R
rare jobs, 23–24
Ray, Michael, on hard work, 4
reading statistics, 48
research, 99–100
respect, winning, 88
respecting others, 171
resumes, 106
Rich Dad, Poor Dad (Kiyosaki), 166
Richards, Keith, 160
The Richest Man in Babylon (Clason), 166
The Riley Guide (Dikel), 20, 143
Rilke, Ranier Maria, 27
Robbins, Anthony, 151, 159, 175
Robertson, James, 19
Robinson, Adam, 68
Robinson, Eddie, 4, 174
Rockefeller, John D., 29
Rogers, Carl, 96
Rogers, Will, 29
Rohn, Jim, 130, 132, 171
Roosevelt, Teddy, 146
Ross, Steven J., 12
Rubinstein, Arthur, 160
Russell, Leland, 151–152
Ruth, Babe, 163

S
sales/selling principles course, 70
savings, paying yourself first, 166–168
Schuller, Robert, 37
Schutz, Angela, 80
Schwartz, David, 168
Schwarzenegger, Arnold, 37
science fiction, jobs for people who like, 18
Scully, Jennifer, 44
Secretan, Lance, 79
Seinfeld, Jerry, 30
self-esteem, 63–64
Dr. Seuss, 136
Sheehan, George, 141
Sher, Barbara, 15

Sherwood, Ron, 16
Short-Term Job Adventures, 141
Siegel, Bernie, 7, 18
Singleton, John, 31, 159
skill sets, 17
Smeltzer, Ruth, 172
Smith, Patti, 31
Smith, Rebecca, 143
Socher, Karen, 11, 14–15, 65
Software Marketing Corp., 62
software products, 72
Soren, Tabitha, 119
Spectrum Holobyte, 106
speech/business presentation courses, 70
Star, Darren, 16
Star Trek: The Next Generation television show, 18
starting, learning how to begin, 149
Stein, Ben, 163
Steingart, Max, 159
Stephanopoulos, George, 119
Stern, Howard, 22, 123
Sternbach, Rick, 18
Stewart, Jon, 163, 173
Stipe, Michael, 31
stress, 78
study abroad, 53–54
study abroad vignettes
    Buss, Trevver, 52
    De Voe, Tim, 52
    Hughes, Julia, 50, 51
    Oscar Foster, 49–51
    work camps, 52
success, helping others toward, 170–171
Success poem (Emerson), 172
suggestions, being open to, 89
Swanson, Dave, 44
Swartout, Kristy, 20, 139

T
"Take Time" poem, 161
taking chances, 39
Teach for America, 101, 102
teachers, bonus tips for, 177
Temporary Recruiters Association, 127
temporary work, 120
tests, magazine, 12–13
Thau, Richard, 16
Thayer, Harry, 29
"The Making of Jurassic Park" conference, 128–129
The Rules for Being Human, 164–165

The Six Habits of Students Who Will Go Far, 148
Thigpen, Felicia, 117
Think and Grow Rich (Hill), 33
Thinking about Thinking (McKowen), 23
Thompson, David, 54
Thoreau, Henry David, 128
time management, 70, 74–78
Toffler, Alvin, 96
Toms, Justine and Michael, 14
Tonner, Simon, 57–58
Top Ten Reasons You Can Get Your Dream Job, 175
del Toro, Benicio, 43
Tracy, Brian, 39
trade journals, 97–98
TransUnion Corporation, 132
Trobetsky, Darron, 142–144, 145
The Truth About College (Edelstein), 63
Tuerack, Gary, 64, 80
Turgenev, Ivan, 144
Turner, Tina, 24
Twain, Mark, 31, 43, 61, 133
Tyson, Eric, 136

U
U2, 30, 33
The Ultimate New Employee Survival Guide (Holton), 142
Union Carbide, 103
uniqueness, 152–153
Unlimited Power (Robbins), 151
unusual jobs, 23–24

V
Van Dyke, Henry, 83
Van Gogh, Vincent, 18, 137
"Very Seriously Fun Work," 23
video games, jobs for people who like, 19
visualization, 138
"Volkswagen Bug" phenomenon, 152
Vonnegut, Kurt, 39

W
Waitley, Denis, 26, 130, 136, 137, 138, 153
Wall Street Journal, 26
Walpole, Hugh, 158
Walton, Sam, 168

Ward, William Arthur, 55
Ware, Eugene, 88
Warhol, Andy, 83
Washington, Booker T., 169
Waters, Mike, 73
The Wealthy Barber (Chilton), 45, 166
websites for success, 180
websites
  Association Job Source Index, 19
  Company Info Guide, 20
  JobStar Career, 19
  Occupational Outlook Handbook, 19
  The Riley Guide, 20
  www.passionpuzzle.com, 14

Westerburg, Paul, 40
Wharton School of Business, three-step success technique, 137–138
What Color is Your Parachute? (Bolles), 144
What Is the What, 55
White, E.B., 155
White, Willye B., 99
Williams, Robin, 31
Winfrey, Oprah, 5, 31, 32, 42, 119, 162, 172
Winsor, Kathleen, 63
Woods, Tiger, 160
work camps, 52
working experience, lack of, 17

Workplace Values, 35
worthiness, 88–89
Wozniak, Steve, 66
Wright, Charnae, 140, 145
Wright brothers, 38
writing courses, 68–69

Y

You Are Smarter Than You Think (Mollan-Masters), 72
Young, Eva, 77

Z

Zucker, David, 167